MOTION PICTURES AND YOUTH: A SUMMARY

GETTING IDEAS FROM THE MOVIES

MOTION PICTURES AND YOUTH

THE PAYNE FUND STUDIES

W. W. Charters, Chairman

Motion Pictures and Youth: A Summary, by W. W. Charters, Director, Bureau of Educational Research, Ohio State University.

Combined with

Getting Ideas from the Movies, by P. W. Holaday, Indianapolis Public Schools, and George D. Stoddard, Director, Iowa Child Welfare Research Station.

Motion Pictures and the Social Attitudes of Children, by Ruth C. Peterson and L. L. Thurstone, Department of Psychology, University of Chicago.

Combined with

The Social Conduct and Attitudes of Movie Fans, by Frank K. Shuttleworth and Mark A. May, Institute of Human Relations, Yale University.

The Emotional Responses of Children to the Motion Picture Situation, by W. S. Dysinger and Christian A. Ruckmick, Department of Psychology, State University of Iowa.

Combined with

Motion Pictures and Standards of Morality, by Charles C. Peters, Professor of Education, Pennsylvania State College.

Children's Sleep, by Samuel Renshaw, Vernon L. Miller, and Dorothy Marquis, Department of Psychology, Ohio State University.

Movies and Conduct, by Herbert Blumer, Department of Sociology, University of Chicago.

The Content of Motion Pictures, by Edgar Dale, Research Associate, Bureau of Educational Research, Ohio State University.

Combined with

Children's Attendance at Motion Pictures, by Edgar Dale.

Movies, Delinquency, and Crime, by Herbert Blumer and Philip M. Hauser, Department of Sociology, University of Chicago.

Boys, Movies, and City Streets, by Paul G. Cressey and Frederick M. Thrasher, New York University.

How to Appreciate Motion Pictures, by Edgar Dale, Research Associate, Bureau of Educational Research, Ohio State University.

MOTION PICTURES AND YOUTH

A SUMMARY

❖

W. W. CHARTERS

DIRECTOR, BUREAU OF EDUCATIONAL RESEARCH,
OHIO STATE UNIVERSITY

NEW YORK
THE MACMILLAN COMPANY
1933

THIS SERIES OF TWELVE STUDIES OF THE
INFLUENCE OF MOTION PICTURES UPON
CHILDREN AND YOUTH HAS BEEN MADE BY
THE COMMITTEE ON EDUCATIONAL RE-
SEARCH OF THE PAYNE FUND AT THE RE-
QUEST OF THE NATIONAL COMMITTEE FOR
THE STUDY OF SOCIAL VALUES IN MOTION
PICTURES, NOW THE MOTION PICTURE RE-
SEARCH COUNCIL, 366 MADISON AVENUE,
NEW YORK CITY. THE STUDIES WERE DE-
SIGNED TO SECURE AUTHORITATIVE AND
IMPERSONAL DATA WHICH WOULD MAKE
POSSIBLE A MORE COMPLETE EVALUATION
OF MOTION PICTURES AND THEIR SOCIAL
POTENTIALITIES

CHAIRMAN'S PREFACE

MOTION PICTURES are not understood by the present generation of adults. They are new; they make an enormous appeal to children; and they present ideas and situations which parents may not like. Consequently when parents think of the welfare of their children who are exposed to these compelling situations, they wonder about the effect of the pictures upon the ideals and behavior of the children. Do the pictures really influence children in any direction? Are their conduct, ideals, and attitudes affected by the movies? Are the scenes which are objectionable to adults understood by children, or at least by very young children? Do children eventually become sophisticated and grow superior to pictures? Are the emotions of children harmfully excited? In short, just what effect do motion pictures have upon children of different ages?

Each individual has his answer to these questions. He knows of this or that incident in his own experience, and upon these he bases his conclusions. Consequently opinions differ widely. No one in this country up to the present time has known in any general and impersonal manner just what effect motion pictures have upon children. Meanwhile children clamor to attend the movies as often as they are allowed to go. Moving pictures make a profound appeal to children of all ages. In such a situation it is obvious that a comprehensive study of the influence of motion pictures upon children and youth is appropriate.

To measure these influences the investigators who cooperated to make this series of studies analyzed the problem

v

to discover the most significant questions involved. They set up individual studies to ascertain the answer to the questions and to provide a composite answer to the central question of the nature and extent of these influences. In using this technique the answers must inevitably be sketches without all the details filled in; but when the details are added the picture will not be changed in any essential manner. Parents, educators, and physicians will have little difficulty in fitting concrete details of their own into the outlines which these studies supply.

Specifically, the studies were designed to form a series to answer the following questions: What sorts of scenes do the children of America see when they attend the theaters? How do the mores depicted in these scenes compare with those of the community? How often do children attend? How much of what they see do they remember? What effect does what they witness have upon their ideals and attitudes? Upon their sleep and health? Upon their emotions? Do motion pictures directly or indirectly affect the conduct of children? Are they related to delinquency and crime, and, finally, how can we teach children to discriminate between movies that are artistically and morally good and bad?

The history of the investigations is brief. In 1928 William H. Short, Executive Director of the Motion Picture Research Council, invited a group of university psychologists, sociologists, and educators to meet with the members of the Council to confer about the possibility of discovering just what effect motion pictures have upon children, a subject, as has been indicated, upon which many conflicting opinions and few substantial facts were in existence. The university men proposed a program of study. When Mr. Short appealed to The Payne Fund for a grant to support such an investigation, he found the foundation receptive because of its well-known interest in motion pictures as one of the major influences in the lives of modern youth. When the appropriation had been made the investigators organized themselves into a Committee on Educational Research of The Payne Fund with the following membership: L. L. Thurstone, Frank N. Freeman, R. E. Park, Herbert Blumer, Philip M. Hauser of the University of Chicago; George D. Stoddard, Christian A. Ruckmick, P. W. Holaday, and Wendell Dysinger of the University of Iowa; Mark A. May and Frank K. Shuttleworth of Yale University; Frederick M. Thrasher and Paul G. Cressey of New York University; Charles C. Peters of Pennsylvania State College; Ben D. Wood of Columbia University; and Samuel Renshaw, Edgar Dale, and W. W. Charters of Ohio State University. The investigations have extended through four years, 1929–1932, inclusive.

The committee's work is an illustration of an interesting technique for studying any social problem. The distinctive characteristic of this technique is to analyze a complex social problem into a series of subordinate problems, to select competent investigators to work upon each of the subordinate projects and to integrate the findings of all the investigators as a solution of the initial problem. Such a program yields a skeleton framework, which, while somewhat lacking in detail, is substantially correct if the contributing investigations have been validly conducted. To provide this framework or outline is the task of research. To fill in the detail and to provide the interpretations are the natural and easy tasks of those who use the data.

W. W. C.

Ohio State University
September, 1933

MOTION PICTURES AND YOUTH

The Initiation of the Studies

At the initial meeting of the investigators with the Motion Picture Research Council they found that the Council had a comprehensive group of problems upon which they were seeking data for the development of a national policy concerning motion pictures. Later these were formulated as a series of two score questions relating to the effect of motion pictures upon children, youth, adults, and communities; the effect of current motion pictures upon the impressions that foreign countries gain of the United States; how well the motion-picture industry is organized to perform its social responsibilities; what may be accomplished through governmental agencies to control the effects of the motion pictures; and how a campaign of education may be organized to produce socially desirable results.

The investigators first proceeded to eliminate certain areas of study indicated in the questions with which they were not competent to deal. Specifically they were not equipped to discover what attitudes toward American life current motion pictures were creating abroad. While this problem would easily yield to investigation it involved a separate organization and a substantial subsidy. A study of the financial, legal, economic, and administrative virtues and vices of the motion-picture industry was not undertaken because this problem belonged primarily in the field of economics and business while our group of investigators were psychologists, sociologists, and educators. Nor did the group investigate and assemble methods of educating the public with regard to the control of motion pictures beyond the preparation of materials on motion-picture appreciation and criticism for the use of high-school students. These studies will be undertaken for the Motion Picture Research Council by competent investigators when the depression lifts.

The investigators did feel, however, that they would enjoy the opportunity to assemble data in answer to a number of the other questions proposed.

The Council asked, "What is the amount of knowledge gained and retained from motion pictures by children of various ages and the types of the knowledge most likely to be thus gained and retained?" Holaday and Stoddard have answered the first half of the question quite adequately and with four others of the group have indicated an answer to the second half.

The Council also wanted to know "the extent to which motion pictures influence the conduct of children and youth either in desirable or undesirable directions and particularly in regard to patterns of sex behavior." Blumer in his conduct study, Blumer and Hauser in their delinquency study, and Cressey and Thrasher have assembled massive and significant data upon this question.

What effect motion pictures have upon the attitudes of children toward significant social concepts, standards, and ideals of children was a matter of concern to the Council. Upon this point data have been assembled by Peterson and Thurstone and by May and Shuttleworth.

We were asked to discover the effect of motion pictures upon the health of children. While no direct attack was made upon the problem an interesting indirect attack was

developed by Renshaw, Miller, and Marquis, in the study
of the influence of motion-picture attendance upon restless-
ness in sleep which is in turn related to the health of children.

The Council also wished to know whether or not motion
pictures influenced the emotions of children and whether
this influence if established was exerted in wholesome or in
harmful ways. Upon the first half of this problem a study
was made by Dysinger and Ruckmick; on the second half
data were assembled by Blumer and Hauser and by Cressey
and Thrasher.

The Council raised a number of questions concerning the
effect of current commercial films upon the standards of
American life. It wanted to know "the characteristics of
good motion pictures in the opinion of different intelligence
levels and social groups" and was concerned about the
respects in which current pictures shown in commercial
theaters measured up to or offended against these standards.
These questions were studied directly by Peters, who developed techniques for the investigation of the problem and
used them on four types of content.

Of major interest to the Council was an analysis of the
content of current films. It felt that if it were proved that
children acquired information, changed attitudes, and
modified conduct as a result of movie attendance the directions in which these changes occurred would be determined by what they saw in the movies. Dale analyzed the
content of several hundred films and classified the types of
scenes which were presented.

The Council wished also to know the number of children
by ages who attended motion-picture theaters and the frequency with which they made their visits. This information
was collected by Dale.

Finally the Council was interested in knowing what could

be done to teach children to discriminate between good and poor movies. In studying this problem Dale produced a text-book on motion-picture appreciation for high-school children.

Some questions in this area were not answered. We did not rank the motion pictures in a scale of influence in relation to other agencies such as the home, the school, the church, and the press. To rank these factors according to greater or less in-fluence with objective accuracy is impossible with any known techniques. It is apparent in the interpretations of Blumer, Thrasher, May, and others that many agencies exert an in-fluence upon children and that of these the movies are one.

The investigators sought to find data, but could not, to prove that the onset of puberty is or is not affected by motion pictures. (The age of the onset of puberty had not been fixed in scientific studies prior to the advent of the movies.) They were asked to find out whether or not mo-tion pictures stifled the imagination of children, healthfully stimulated it, over-stimulated its action, or whether their effects were greater or less than that of books. These ques-tions we did not investigate. Although the Council wished to know whether or not our findings for children were valid for adults we confined our attention for the most part to children and youth and used adults only occasionally for comparison in specific cases.

Summarizing, we may say that instead of attacking in-dividually each of a score or more of the questions proposed, the investigators set up a few basic studies which when completed would provide data for answering completely or in part a wide range of separate queries.

THE PLAN OF THE STUDIES

THE studies fall naturally into two groups: one, to measure the effect of motion pictures as such upon children and youth; the other, to study current motion-picture content and children's attendance at commercial movie theaters to see what they come in contact with when they attend them.

In measuring the effect of pictures upon children the studies were focused on influences upon behavior and conduct. Proceeding from this objective by analysis it was logical to set up studies of information, attitudes, health, and emotions as well as upon one-to-one correspondence between motion pictures and child behavior. This is a logical procedure because behavior may safely be assumed to be influenced by what one knows, by his attitudes, by his emotions, and by the condition of his health.

Then on the basis of what is discovered to be the effect of motion pictures upon these five areas—information, attitudes, emotions, health, and conduct—it is possible to gauge the effect of current commercial motion pictures upon children by ascertaining two facts: what they see when they attend the theaters and how often they go. If, in short, the general influence of motion pictures is ascertained, if the content is known and the number of visits of children has been computed, the total influence of the pictures will be in general a product of these three factors. That is to say, if motion pictures have any influence upon children, if the pictures are good and if the attendance is optimally spaced we can assume that the influence upon behavior will be beneficial. If motion pictures have no influence it will not matter from that point of view whether children go to the movies or not nor what they see when they go. If, however, an influence is discovered, if the pictures are bad, and if children attend the theater we may reasonably assume that the influence upon conduct will be harmful.

The major interest of the investigators was directed to the measurement of influence because it is important to know that pictures do or do not exhibit potency without respect to goodness or badness. If it is established that children are moved by pictures toward dislike for one social value and toward liking for another, and if it is shown that both facts and errors are learned and remembered, it is apparent that motion pictures have fundamental influences which may be exerted in any direction. The range and limits of the potency of motion pictures are of major significance to educators and are fundamental to the drawing of inferences in a very large number of areas.

The interest of the investigators in the content of the current motion-picture situation was minor in the sense that if movies should permanently exert a strong influence upon a variety of social standards and activities the current pictures can be changed in tone and attitude with much greater ease in the long view than can the psychological and educational effects of pictures as such. If the influence of the motion picture can be measured, validated, and interpreted with accuracy the formulas so obtained can be applied to all pictures to discover with validity whether they are having beneficial or harmful effects upon children. They become measuring instruments to apply to the movies which are now being exhibited or with equal propriety to the pictures which will supplant the current films.

Yet while some investigators were primarily interested in establishing measuring instruments because of their usefulness as measures to be used on all kinds of pictures, others were concerned about the effect of the current run of pictures in the commercial theater upon the present generation of children and youth. And by combining the factors studied we are able to provide an indication of the influence of current commercial films upon the behavior of individuals and the standards of communities.

Finally, the group worked as individuals to provide answers to specific fundamental questions. They did not attempt to draw general conclusions from all the studies. The chairman, however, was given the commission of making the following interpretation of the findings for the consideration of the Motion Picture Research Council and the information of the public.

LEARNING FACTS

How much information children acquire from the movies is a question of interest to parents and is a matter of concern to them when their children view pictures which the parents do not like. In the latter case, the problem is accompanied by fear if the parent believes that his children learn much from the picture and is dismissed lightly if he thinks that most of what they see passes over their heads.

To the question of how much children retain of what is in a picture for them to see, Holaday and Stoddard directed their attention in a three-year study.[1] They used seventeen commercial pictures such as "Tom Sawyer," "New Moon," "Stolen Heaven," "Rango," "Passion Flower," and "Fighting Caravans." Somewhat over 3,000 children and adults participated in the study as observers. They were selected in four age groups which were all given the same tests upon the information acquired. These tests were of two types, one testing the retention of the plot of the story—the actions and sayings of the actors,—the other testing the general information of historical, geographical, or mechanical items. To the 3,000 individuals were administered a total of 26 tests each containing from 30 to 64 factual items and producing an aggregate of more than 20,000 testings for a total of 813,000 items attempted. Proper precautions were

[1] *Getting Ideas from the Movies*, by P. W. Holaday and George D. Stoddard.

taken to equate groups for age, intelligence, and the like so that the results from group to group might be comparable. Careful statistical techniques were utilized.

The most striking conclusion translated roughly into concrete language is this. If parents take their 8 year old child to the movies he will catch three out of every five items that the parents catch. This conclusion is arrived at somewhat as follows. The next day after viewing each of six pictures in 1930 to 1931 and answering a total of approximately 400 carefully selected questions dealing with items appearing in the scenes, 162 "superior" adults— young college professors, graduate students and their wives —made a score of 87.8 out of a possible 100. At the same time 959 children in grades 2 and 3 made a score of 52.5. Coincidentally 1,180 children in grades 5 and 6 made a score of 65.9 and youths in grades 9 and 10 achieved a score of 80.9. Thus using the adult score as a basis, children of 8 and 9 years made 60 per cent, those of 11 and 12 made 75 per cent, and children of 15 and 16 made 91 per cent of the score obtained by adults. Hence roughly speaking a parent who is a superior adult can count upon his young child to see approximately 3 out of the 5 things he sees, his 11 or 12 year old child to see 3 out of 4, and his 15 or 16 year old to catch 9 out of 10. Or putting the conclusion in another way the 8 or 9 year old sees half of what is to be seen, the 11 or 12 year old two thirds, and the 15 or 16 year old four fifths of what is to be seen. This is true if we assume, as a reading of the study demonstrates, that the questions in the tests are a reasonably fair sample of the questions that might be asked. The amount of information acquired is very high.

A second interesting fact relates to the surprising amount the children remember about a picture six weeks and three months later. In general the second-third-grade children at the end of six weeks remember 90 per cent of what they knew on the day following the show. Three months after seeing the picture they remember as much as they did six weeks after seeing it. In some cases, as with "Tom Sawyer," they remember more at the end of six weeks and still more at the end of three months. At all ages including the adults the slow drop of the curve of forgetting is striking. The investigators conclude from the data that the "curves of retention are considerably higher than those obtained by previous investigators (using other materials) and motion pictures appear to make a greater contribution to visual education than was previously suspected." [2]

Of interest is an implication lying within the fact that very young children remember correctly 50 or 60 per cent of what they see. Conversely this means that they do not get 50 or 40 per cent of what they see. When they do not answer questions accurately it may not mean that their memories are blank on those points. They may have acquired misinformation. Dysinger and Ruckmick found in their interviews that children frequently misunderstood the meaning of what they had seen and thereby reacted in unexpected fashion at their "reading points."

A third interesting fact of educational significance drawn from the study is this. Children of all ages tend to accept as authentic what they see in the movies. Thus pre-tests on general information were given to groups and their scores were computed. Then equated groups viewed pictures in which were shown the errors of fact which had been covered in the pre-tests. The two sets of scores were compared and it was found that at each of the three age levels the incorrectly shown items had left their marks. The children had

---

[2] When quotation marks are used they inclose the statements of the investigators.

increased their fund of knowledge on the correctly shown items covered by the test, but their acceptance of the incorrect items as correct had lowered their improvement in their total scores. They tended to accept the errors as facts. In general "children accept the information in the movies as correct unless it is flagrantly incorrect."

It is of interest to know the types of fact that children remember best. The investigators divided the facts into ten classes and found that "action was remembered best when it concerned sports, general conversation, crime, and fighting, when it had a high emotional tonus and when it occurred in a familiar type of surrounding such as home, school, or tenement. . . . It was understood least when it concerned unfamiliar activities such as bootlegging and business, when it had practically no emotional tonus, and when it occurred in surroundings of an unfamiliar and interesting type such as café and frontier."

The types of information tested in this study are supplemented by the Blumer and Thrasher [3] studies. They analyze the rôle of the movies as a source of information which is noticed and copied by adolescents. In their studies they mass cases covering a wide variety of areas in which information is acquired and used: hints on how to beautify one's self and wear one's clothes, examples of attractive mannerisms, and demonstrations of satisfying love techniques. To these they add patterns for the play of children, suggestions for delinquent action and crime upon occasion. None of these was measured by Blumer and Thrasher with the Holaday-Stoddard techniques, but it may reasonably be assumed that the acquisition of facts in these specific areas described by Blumer and Thrasher proceeds with the

[3] *Movies and Conduct*, by Herbert Blumer: *Motion Pictures, Delinquency, and Crime*, by Herbert Blumer and Philip M. Hauser; *Boys, Movies, and City Streets*, by Paul G. Cressey and Frederick M. Thrasher.

same effectiveness as in the areas studied by Holaday and Stoddard.

Finally no significant sex differences appeared in the amount of information acquired or the amount remembered at later dates. Girls and boys remember about equally well.

In summary Holaday and Stoddard have shown that the amount of information gained from motion pictures by children of all ages including the 8 and 9 year olds is "tremendously high." This constitutes the first link in the sequential chain of the inquiry into the influence of motion pictures upon children and youth.

DEVELOPING ATTITUDES

BECAUSE a close relationship between the attitude of an individual and his actions may be assumed, the study of the effect of motion pictures upon the attitude of children toward important social values is central in importance. The investigations of May and Shuttleworth and of Peterson and Thurstone are consequently interesting links in the chain of studies. May and Shuttleworth [4] conducted two studies: one on the correlation between movie attendance and character and another on the relation of attendance to attitudes toward objects of social interest.

In the first study they selected in three communities 102 children who attended the movies from four to five times a week and 101 other children who attended about twice a month. Each group was about equally divided between boys and girls. The groups were equated for age, sex, school grade, intelligence, occupational level of the father, and cultural home background.

The "movie" and "non-movie" children were compared as to reputation in school among teachers and classmates.

[4] *The Social Conduct and Attitudes of Movie Fans*, by Frank K. Shuttleworth and Mark A. May.

Reputation was measured by six factors: deportment; scholastic work; a conduct record (consisting of tests on coöperation, reliability, persistence, and the like); a check list of descriptive adjectives marked by teachers; a "Guess Who" instrument in which children told who among their classmates met certain specified qualifications; and a "Best Friend" device by which children indicated those among their classmates who were their best friends.

The investigators report: "We have found that the movie children average lower deportment records, do on the average poorer work in their school subjects, are rated lower in reputation by teachers on two rating forms, are rated lower by their classmates on the 'Guess Who' test, are less coöperative and less controlled as measured both by ratings and conduct tests, are slightly more deceptive in school situations, are slightly less skillful in judging what is the most useful and helpful and sensible thing to do, and are slightly less emotionally stable. Against this long record, the movie children are superior on only two measures: They are mentioned more frequently on the 'Guess Who' test as a whole and are named more frequently as best friends by their classmates. Tests showing no differences also need cataloging. These include honesty rating and honesty as measured in out-of-school situations, persistence, suggestibility, and moral knowledge."

Cressey and Thrasher [5] in their study of a congested area in New York City found conditions of similar import. Of 949 boys studied in the area about one quarter were retarded and another quarter were accelerated in school. Of those who attended the movies 4 times a week or more 19 per cent were accelerated in school, 24 per cent were normal, and 57 per cent were retarded. Of those, however,

[5] *Boys, Movies, and City Streets*, by Paul G. Cressey and Frederick M. Thrasher.

who attended once a week or less 35 per cent were accelerated, 33 per cent were normal, and 32 per cent were retarded. The movie group contained nearly twice as many retarded pupils and half as many accelerated pupils as the non-movie children.

Cressey and Thrasher also discovered in this area that among 1,356 boys 109 were delinquents. Of these 22 per cent attended the movies 3 times or more a week and 6 per cent attended less than once a week, while among those who were not delinquent 14 per cent attended 3 times or more a week and 6 per cent attended less than once a week. These figures indicate that for this population there is a positive relationship between truancy and delinquency and frequent movie attendance.

An important question arises at this point. Does extreme movie attendance lead to conduct which harms reputation or do children of low reputation go frequently to the movies? It rises also at other points. Thrasher and Blumer and their associates as they present their cases are faced by the same question and discuss it. The authors who raise the question express the general conclusion that a simple cause and effect relationship does not prevail. To say that the movies are solely responsible for anti-social conduct, delinquency, or crime is not valid. To assert contrariwise that delinquents and criminals happen to frequent the movies and are not affected by them is clearly indefensible. Validity probably rests with a combination of the two—tendencies toward unapproved conduct and movie influence work together to produce more movie interest on the one hand and more anti-social conduct on the other. The two factors drive toward progressive aggravation of unhealthful conditions.

Turning from their conduct study to their attitudes

study, we find that May and Shuttleworth searched diligently for specific criticisms of the movies in literature, in conversation, and the like, and divided them into twelve classes: heroes and boobs of the movies, the people of other lands, prohibition, crime and criminals, sex attitudes, attitude toward schools, clothing, militarism, personal attitude, escape from threatening danger, special dislikes, and a miscellaneous group. For each of the first eleven classes an hypothesis was advanced concerning the effect of the movies upon that particular area. The responsibility of the investigators was to find out whether or not this hypothesis was true. For instance, for the class, heroes and boobs of the movies, the investigators selected the hypothesis that there is a tendency for the movies to place certain characters in a favorable light and to hold up others to ridicule. Their task was to discover whether or not this hypothesis was correct; that is, whether movie and non-movie children showed significant differences in their attitudes toward characters shown in the movies, athletes, Protestant ministers, actors, cowboys, college professors, policemen, and the like.

To explore the eleven hypotheses of which the foregoing is an illustration approximately 250 questions were prepared, making an average of about 22 questions in each area. They thus covered by this procedure all the statements that they could discover about the influence of the movies upon attitudes.

The investigators then selected from large populations of children groups which attended the movies frequently and others which attended them infrequently. The movie groups attended the theater nearly three times a week while the non-movie groups attended less than once a month. Unfortunately, enough children could not be found for their uses who had never attended the movies. The investigators were compelled, therefore, to use children in the groups who had gone to the movies twice a month or less. But the movie group had attended twelve times as often as the other group. Four hundred sixteen movie cases and 443 non-movie cases were studied. These groups were equated for age, school grade, intelligence, socio-economic-educational background, and a few other special factors in individual localities. Equal proportions of boys and girls were included. To each of the groups, movie and non-movie, were given series of statements upon which it was thought there might be discernible differences which might possibly be attributed to movie attendance. These statements occurred usually in the form: "All Most Many Some Few No Chinese are cunning and underhand." Each child was then required to underline one word which best expressed his attitude toward the Chinese. Questions were also used such as, "Which would you rather be, a college professor or a cowboy?" Some true-false statements were included, as "Most Russians are kind and generous." The replies were then tabulated for the movie and the non-movie groups and the differences were observed to see whether or not they were statistically significant.

On the basis of the questions and statements used, no significant differences in attitude were discovered between the movie and non-movie groups on a number of objects including athletics, the Chinese, robbers, gang leaders, rum runners, prohibition agents, prohibition enforcement, the success of marriage, sex attitudes, and the like. Significant differences were found in that movie children admire cowboys, popular actors, dancers, and chorus girls while non-movie children are more interested in such types as the medical student and the college professor. Movie children are more inclined to believe that much drinking and violation of the prohibition laws exist. Movie children set special value on smart clothes and dressing well. They are also more sensitive about parental control. The movie children go to more dances and read more; but the quality of their reading is not high.

They say in conclusion: "That the movies exert an influence there can be no doubt. But it is our opinion that this influence is specific for a given child and a given movie. The same picture may influence different children in distinctly opposite directions. Thus in a general survey such as we have made, the net effect appears small. We are also convinced that among the most frequent attendants the movies are drawing children who are in some way maladjusted and whose difficulties are relieved only in the most temporary manner and are, in fact, much aggravated. In other words, the movies tend to fix and further establish the behavior patterns and types of attitudes which already exist among those who attend most frequently."

This attitude study of May and Shuttleworth is of peculiar interest because it is the only one in which the influence of the motion picture is not clearly apparent either as cause or effect or as an aggravation of precedent conditions. Superficially one might claim that this study indicates that motion pictures have no influence upon boys and girls. That position May and Shuttleworth do not take. They say that movies do exert an influence upon children and indicate that this influence is greater than appears on the surface. The studies of Stoddard, Thurstone, Blumer, Thrasher, and their associates support this position with a huge mass of specific data.

The causes of this neutral effect are several. May says "We were conducting a survey and not an experiment;

we were not attempting to measure attitudes precisely but rather to sample them widely; we recognized that specific undesirable effects may be cancelled by specific desirable effects and that the desirable net effects may be cancelled by some other agency." They advance the theory also that the influence of motion pictures "is specific for a given movie." This is supported by Renshaw, Ruckmick, and other investigators. Other factors operate to produce neutrality.

The measuring instrument of attitudes used in their survey was not so sensitive as that of Peterson and Thurstone which showed positive effects with specific pictures. Peterson-Thurstone scales utilized 25 to 30 units integrated into a total product; the May-Shuttleworth techniques used single units which were considered as disparate items and were not integrated into a single scale of attitudes. The relative results of the survey techniques of May and Shuttleworth and of the experimental techniques of Peterson and Thurstone are roughly analogous to the determination of bodily temperature by the hand and by a thermometer. Fine significant differences which may be read on the thermometer may not be perceived by the hand.

The May-Shuttleworth study is of chief value as a caution. It indicates clearly that the influence of a motion picture is only one of several influences and the attitudes of children are a product of many influences. Native temperament, past experience, family ideals, school instruction, community mores, all theoretically have an effect. The movies themselves conflict with one another in the direction of their influence—a good picture may be followed by a bad, an anti-Chinese film may be neutralized by a pro-Chinese movie. Results may be produced by the influences of other factors. The home influence may be stronger than the movie in specific cases. School instruction may neutralize the influence of a picture. Sometimes the movie may crash through and overpower the influence of the home, the school, or the community.

The total effect of all these influences on the child is analogous to the total effect of an orchestra upon an audience. The violins, the flutes, the brasses contribute to the total orchestral effect. Which instrument is of most importance in the orchestra is an academic question. But a lover of music is much concerned about any one of the instruments which produces sour notes. He demands a workmanlike contribution from every player. So with the movies, the lover of children is concerned with the question of how well the commercial motion picture plays its individual part in the education of children and not with whether it is more or less important than another instrument.

Peterson and Thurstone by the use of different techniques isolated the influence of specific pictures upon groups of children while keeping constant the factors of community standards, habits of children, school influence, home training, and the like. They assumed that these had not materially influenced the children in the brief period between their first and second tests of attitudes; the factor that had changed during the period was exposure to a specific film.

These investigators used eleven highly sensitive instruments to discover changes in attitude toward or against the following eight social objects: the Germans (a scale and a paired comparison), war, (two scales) crime, prohibition, the Chinese, capital punishment, the punishment of criminals (two scales), and the Negro. The instruments were scales which consisted of approximately thirty statements each expressing an attitude toward an object. These statements varied in intensity of position from one extreme of attitude against the object to the other extreme of attitude in favor of the object. The statements were weighted according to techniques described in the study [6] and a total score was computed for each individual to express his attitude toward an object.

The scales were given to high-school children shortly before a picture was seen and the position of the group upon the scale was computed. The picture (which in all cases the children had not seen before) was shown and approximately the day after the showing the scale was given again. The new position of the groups was computed and the resulting change in position noted. In some cases the scale was again checked by some of the groups after two and one-half, five, eight, and nineteen months had clapsed to determine the permanence of the changes which were noted the day after the showing of the picture.

Approximately 4,000 individuals participated in the study as subjects. Most of the subjects were junior and senior high-school students. The exceptions were three in number. In one study 246 college students were used and in another about 100 fourth- and fifth-grade children checked the scale while in three other studies sixth-grade children were included with the junior and senior high-school students. The children were located in the schools of small towns in the neighborhood of Chicago and at Mooseheart, the children's home supported by the Loyal Order of Moose. Small towns were chosen primarily because of the ease of selecting pictures which had not been seen by the children.

Thirteen pictures were selected which met three criteria: they definitely pertained to the issues to be studied, they

[6] *Motion Pictures and the Social Attitudes of Children*, by Ruth C. Peterson and L. L. Thurstone.

were free enough from objectionable matter so that high-school principals could be asked to send their students to see them, and they were sufficiently recent to eliminate distractions caused by fashions or photography. Between 600 and 800 pictures of all kinds were reviewed and from them the thirteen used in the studies were selected. This selection represents an attempt to secure films which would in the judgment of the reviewers be likely to produce a noticeable change in attitude if changes were produced by any pictures. All, however, were well-known films. The titles and issues were: "Four Sons" (on the Germans and war); "Street of Chance" (gambling); "Hide Out" (prohibition); "Son of the Gods" (the Chinese); "Welcome Danger" (the Chinese); "The Valiant" (capital punishment); "Journey's End" (war); "All Quiet on the Western Front" (war); "The Criminal Code" (punishment of criminals); "Alibi" (punishment of criminals); "The Birth of a Nation" (the Negro); "Big House" (punishment of criminals); and "Numbered Men" (punishment of criminals).

The outstanding contribution of the study is the establishment of the fact that the attitude of children toward a social value can be measurably changed by one exposure to a picture. An outstanding picture of potency in its influence upon attitude was "Son of the Gods," a picture selected because it was thought to be favorable to the Chinese. Prior to the showing of the picture the mean attitude of a population of 182 children from grades 9 to 12 inclusive stood at 6.72 on a scale in which the extreme positions were approximately 3.5 at the favorable end of the scale and 9.5 at the unfavorable end. After the children had seen the picture the mean shifted 1.22 steps in a favorable direction from 6.72 to 5.50 and this difference was 17.5 times the probable error of the differences. The shift in attitude is "very striking." "The Birth of a Nation" was shown to 434 children of grades 6 to 12 inclusive. Prior to the showing the mean position of this population was 7.41 with extremes of approximately 2.5 at the unfavorable end of the scale to approximately 9.5 at the favorable end. After exposure to the picture the position shifted in an unfavorable direction to 5.93 with a difference of 1.48, which was 25.5 times the probable error of the differences. This was the largest shift obtained in the studies. "All Quiet on the Western Front" produced in 214 junior and senior high-school students a shift against war 14.98 times the probable error of the differences and "The Criminal Code" a shift against the punishment of criminals 12.2 times the probable error of the difference with 246 college students and 11.7 times against the same issue with 276 high-school students. These were the outstanding cases. Significant results were obtained, also, from the showing of "Four Sons" upon attitude toward the Germans, "Welcome Danger," "The Valiant," and "All Quiet on the Western Front." Statistically important changes did not result from single showings of "Four Sons" upon the attitude toward war, of "Hide Out" toward prohibition, of "Journey's End," with one group, toward war, and "Alibi," "Big House," and "Numbered Men" toward the punishment of criminals. In all of these cases but one the differences, however, were in the expected direction. In "Street of Chance" the investigators expected to discover a change of attitude favorable to gambling but a significant change against gambling was recorded.

The range of influence of the motion picture is sensibly broadened by a second fact which these attitude studies have discovered. The investigators found that the effect of pictures upon attitude is cumulative. They demonstrated the fact that two pictures are more powerful than one and three are more potent than two. At Mooseheart, when "Big House" was shown to 138 junior and senior high-school children and "Numbered Men" to another group of 168, neither produced a statistically significant shift in attitude toward the punishment of criminals. When both pictures were seen by a group the change became significant. The shift was then 3.0 times the probable error of the differences. When to these two exposures was added exposure to a third film on the same subject, "The Criminal Code," the shift was still greater and amounted to 6.7 times the probable error.

Again at Mooseheart "Journey's End" and "All Quiet on the Western Front" were shown separately and in combination. These pictures had individual potency. "Journey's End" alone caused a shift of 5.07 times the probable error against war and "All Quiet on the Western Front" produced one of 6.07 times in the same direction. When the former was followed by the latter the shift was increased to 8.07 times the probable error and when the latter was followed by the former the amount of change was increased to 8.26 times.

This pair of studies indicates a significant hypothesis, namely, that even though one picture related to a social issue may not significantly affect the attitude of an individual or a group, continued exposure to pictures of similar character will in the end produce a measurable change of attitude. What the range and limits of such influence may be we do not know. Whether or not it is true in this area that the repetitions of exposure would increase indefinitely is a subject worthy of investigation. Whether or not there is a threshold of personal sensitivity in children above which many pictures do not rise in power and influence we cannot say. But it is worth while to know that under the conditions of these studies at least, the cumulative effect of pictures upon attitudes is unmistakably indicated.

To these two leads into the influence of motion pictures upon attitudes Peterson and Thurstone have added a third. They have shown that the shifts created by exposure to a film have substantial permanence. In six localities the attitude scales were repeated at varying intervals and changes in average positions of the groups were computed. The case of the high school at Geneva, Illinois, is typical. Before seeing the film, "Son of the Gods," the children's position on a scale of attitude toward the Chinese was 6.61 and promptly after seeing the film it was 5.19—a shift in favor of the Chinese. Five months after seeing the film there was a recession to 5.72 toward the original position of 5.19 and nineteen months later the position was 5.76. That is to say, the effect of the film had not worn off in a year and a half. In none of the six localities was the recession complete except in one. At Paxton, Illinois, the original position was 4.34 on the scale of attitude toward war before exposure to the film, "All Quiet on the Western Front." After viewing the picture the group shifted to 3.74, indicating a less favorable attitude toward war. Eight months later the position had changed to 4.64 which is more favorable to war than was the original attitude. Probably other influences had played upon the children during these eight months. In all other cases residual traces of the exposure were in evidence at the end of periods of two and one-half, four, six, or eight months.

The principle of permanence is indicated by these investigations. One cannot say that the effects of pictures disappear rapidly. And this position is supported in numerous cases reported by Blumer from the movie autobiographies of his subjects, where hundreds of memories of the influence of specific pictures are related in later years by adults. In other cases Blumer's autobiographers, however, attest to the short-lived influence of movies upon conduct.

This trio of conclusions has great significance for education. We can conclude on the basis of fact that single pictures may produce a change in attitude, that the influence of pictures is cumulative, and that their effects are substantially permanent. This is the second link in the chain of evidence.

How to interpret the social significance of these changes is an interesting consideration. One clue is given in the scores upon the scales. For instance, to select one of the more powerful films, before the picture "Son of the Gods" was shown there were individuals in the group at one extreme position of unfavorableness marked 9.5 upon the scale—meaning roughly: "There are no refined or cultured Chinese," "I don't see how any one could ever like the Chinese," or "There is nothing about the Chinese that I like or admire." Six steps to the other extreme in this group were those who held: "I like the Chinese" and "I'd like to know more Chinese people." The mode of the group and the average were slightly unfavorable at 6.72, which is slightly beyond the neutral point of 6 and toward the unfavorable end. The mode (the most common position taken by the individuals in the group) was: "I have no particular love nor hate for the Chinese." After the picture was shown the same spread of six units was in evidence, from 3.5 to 9.5, but there were fewer children at 9.5 and more at 3.5. The change was 1.22 indicating a shift of about 20 per cent of the distance between the positions of the most extreme and the least extreme individuals in the group. The mode had shifted from neutrality to a point between "The Chinese are pretty decent" and "Chinese parents are unusually devoted to their children."

STIMULATING EMOTIONS

LABORATORY techniques and autobiographical case studies were utilized in studying the effect of motion pictures upon the emotions of children. Dysinger and Ruckmick worked with a galvanometer to measure galvanic responses and with the pneumo-cardiograph to measure changes in the circulatory system. They [7] worked with 89 subjects in their laboratory and with 61 subjects in the theaters. In age the subjects ranged from six years to fifty and were divided between those under 11 years; 11 to 12 years; 13 to 15 years; 16 to 18 years; 19 to 25 years; and over 25 years. In the theater under theater conditions they used 61 subjects in three age groups: around 9 years, 16 years, and 22 years. Children of average intelligence were chosen with intelligence quotients between 90 and 110 when available, or with normal age-grade placement in other cases. The subjects were about equally divided between the sexes.

The apparatus was attached to the 150 individual children in the laboratory and in the balcony or the rear seats of theaters. The customary patience of the psychological laboratory technician was amply exercised in this investigation. The records of the reactions of the subjects were taken on films. In numerous cases verbal reports were given by the subject about the points of greatest interest to serve as explanations of the records.

Two types of scene were used: those that depicted dangerous situations and those that contained sex content. In the laboratory the pictures "Hop to it Bell Hop," a slap-

[7] *The Emotional Responses of Children to the Motion-Picture Situation*, by W. S. Dysinger and Christian A. Ruckmick.

stick, "The Iron Mule," a comedy, and "The Feast of Ishtar," an erotic play, were used. In the theaters the subjects viewed "Charlie Chan's Chance," "The Yellow Ticket," "The Road to Singapore," and "His Woman." The reactions of subjects at 187 points for scenes of danger, conflict, or tragedy and at 35 points for suggestive or love scenes were recorded.

The specific contribution to this type of study lies in the fact that the apparatus records very fine reactions when the subject is sitting quietly—looking like a well-mannered, quiet, and well-controlled young boy or girl. It reinforces the impression that one cannot estimate from gross movement of the body or absence of such movement what is happening to an individual. Specifically, it cannot be inferred by a parent sitting beside his quiet child that internal excitement is not occurring as incidents in the screen drama unfold before him.

Among the findings the most significant are three in number. The records show first that scenes of danger, conflict, or tragedy produce the greatest effect as measured by the galvanometer upon the 9 year old group (from 6 to 12 years old); the curve falls rapidly among the 16 year olds (from 13 to 18 years) and is weakest with the adult group (over 19 years). There is a real difference in the reactions from one age level to the next. The reaction of adults is small compared with that of the 9 year olds because of their consciousness of the unreality of the scenes, the quality of the acting, or their ability to forecast what is going to happen.

The records show a second trend in connection with the romantic and erotic scenes. In this case the 9 year olds (6 to 12 years old) are on the average least affected. To be sure, their deflections on the graph are similar in average to those of the adults in one series of experiments and greater than adults in the other; but the investigators point out the likelihood that the danger elements, which in some cases could not be completely eliminated from erotic scenes, account for part of the deflections and this is the more likely because children of this age, according to Holaday and Stoddard, remember only one half to two thirds of what they see and may, therefore, misunderstand some of the scenes. This element of misunderstanding was frequently discovered by Dysinger and Ruckmick among the younger children in their interviews.

The greatest deflections from normal patterns in viewing erotic scenes was located among the 16 year olds (ages 12 to 18). The average is the largest of the three age levels. They are most often extreme, and verbal reports in the interviews seldom mention the factors which influence adults called "adult discount"—the factor of realizing the unreality of the drama, observing the quality of the acting, and the like. Compared with the other groups the 16 year old group gives the most extreme responses.

More specifically the authors report: "Most children of 9 gave very little response [to love scenes]. At 10 some were found to respond. At 11 and 12 others responded. Above 13 there was usually a definite response. The peak in intensity of reaction does not seem to be reached until the age of 16 years."

A third result reported frequently by the investigator is the presence of striking individual differences in children. In "The Feast of Ishtar," for instance, twelve erotic "reading points" were studied. In the 6 to 10 year group two subjects gave only one reading, each above zero. (Zero indicates a merely normal reaction.) However, one boy of 9 years and 2 months gave only one zero reading. He was affected by all the scenes but one. Between these two extremes were others who gave significant responses. Similarly in the 11 to 12 year group one subject gave only zero readings, while another provided only two zero readings. Again in the 13 to 15 year group one subject gave zero readings at all points except where the index was zero-plus, in contrast to another subject only five months older, who gave wide deflections at all the points. In the 16 to 18 year group at 125 reading points there were only 16 zero readings. Here again, however, the subject least affected reacted with seven zero readings in contrast with another who showed violent reactions in all. In the adult group there were many more zero readings than in the 16 year group but a considerable number of large deflections were also found. Similar individual differences were found in the reaction of individuals at all ages to scenes of danger. While in general the reactions to these scenes decreased with age, marked differences were found even among the adults.

It thus appears that while children of ages 6 to 12 are on the average not likely to react to love scenes, individual children in the group will show significant reactions and similarly the 13 to 15 year group will contain individuals who show important reactions. In the 16 to 18 year group it appears that none is free from the influence of love scenes.

A fourth indication of interest is the conclusion of the investigators that there are in this study no clear sex differences in reaction to love scenes. Males and females are equally influenced. Differences within each sex are greater than differences between the sexes.

The Dysinger-Ruckmick study in general establishes the fact that measurable reactions of children to two types of scene—danger and love—can be secured and indicates the significant social conclusion that a few children at the age of nine years react to erotic scenes in motion pictures, and that this reaction occurs in increasing numbers of children until it reaches its climax among the 16 to 18 year olds and thereafter falls away probably through the influence of "adult discount."

By a quite different technique Blumer studied the effects of motion pictures upon the emotional life of children. In seeking to throw light upon this problem Blumer used motion-picture autobiographies supplemented by interviews. The autobiographies were secured from about 1,800 college and high-school students, office workers, and factory workers. Four types of experience were studied: fright, sorrow, love, and excitement. Stating his conclusions in relation to the emotion of fright as typical of the influence of motion pictures upon the four areas, Blumer says that the experience "of fright, horror, or agony as a result of witnessing certain kinds of motion pictures seems common from the accounts of children and of high-school and college students. The experience is most conspicuous in the case of children although it is not infrequently showed by those of greater age. Its manifestations vary from shielding the eyes at crucial scenes during the showing of the pictures to nightmares and terrifying dreams, including sometimes experiences of distinct shock, almost of neurotic proportions."

The extent of the fright among children is "quite large." Of 237 children in the fourth to seventh grades in one school who were asked if they had ever been frightened or horrified by any motion picture 93 per cent answered in the affirmative. Of 458 high-school students who wrote autobiographies 61 per cent mentioned such experiences and 17 per cent said they never had been frightened by pictures.

Among the movie objects which produce fear in the young

are: "spooks, ghosts, phantoms, devils, gorillas, bears, tigers, bandits, 'bad men,' grabbing hands and claws, fighting, shooting, falling or hanging from high places, drownings, wrecks, collisions, fire, and flood."

Expressions of emotions during the witnessing of fearful pictures are such as: biting finger nails, crunching teeth, twisting caps, grabbing one's neighbor, feeling shivery, hiding the eyes until the scene changes, looking away, screaming, jumping out of the seat, and getting under the seat. On the way home fear so induced leads to such actions as: running home, being frightened at shadows, avoiding dark streets, and holding on to others. At home the effects appear as: staying close to mother, looking back of one's chair, fear of going to bed, looking under the bed, closing the window, begging for a light to be left burning, hiding the head under covers, seeing devils dancing in the dark, wanting to sleep with some one, bad dreams, calling out in sleep, sleepwalking, and the like.

Such expressions of fright are ordinarily short-lived. The child regains control of his thoughts and feelings with the passage of time, sometimes by the next day, sometimes in the course of the next few days. But in the case of some individuals fear or fright becomes fixed and lasts for a long time. Blumer does not assess the value or harm of showing such pictures to children and points to the interesting fact that many children like to be frightened by pictures.

Blumer concludes that the sampling of instances of fright, sorrow, love, and excitement provided in his report "suffice to establish the point that motion pictures may play very vividly upon a given emotion of the individual; his impulses may be so aroused and his imagery so fixed that for a period of time he is transported out of his normal conduct and is completely subjugated by his impulses."

These studies establish the third link in the chain of evidence. Holaday and Stoddard show that much information is secured from motion pictures, Peterson and Thurstone establish the forceful influence of a single picture upon attitudes, and Dysinger and Ruckmick and Blumer indicate the considerable influence of the movies upon the emotions of children.

Affecting Sleep

The investigators had two alternatives to consider in studying the possible effects of motion-picture attendance upon health. One was to investigate the direct relationship between movie attendance and health by correlating it with the various physiological indices of health. The other was to study the correlation of theater attendance with motility in sleep and assume an established relationship between the disturbance of sleep patterns and the indices of health. The latter alternative was chosen.

Renshaw, Miller, and Marquis [8] undertook this investigation. Specifically they selected children, ascertained their normal sleep patterns in terms of motility, exposed the children to the movies, and observed the changes in sleep patterns which followed movie attendance. To secure comparative data they measured changes occurring after sleep deprivation in the evening and in the morning, and after drinking coffee or Kaffee Hag in the evening.

To locate children with regular régimes of living in such numbers as to permit of economical study, whose actions could be controlled, and who were near a theater was a difficult task which was fortunately solved by the coöperation of the officials of the Bureau of Juvenile Research in Columbus, Ohio. Briefly the children were of all types,

[8] *Children's Sleep*, by Samuel Renshaw, Vernon L. Miller, and Dorothy P. Marquis.

"good" and "bad," "bright" and "dull," varying in age
from 6 to 19 years, and living under conditions which produce normal happiness.

In the nine experiments conducted by the investigators,
92 boys and 71 girls were used varying in age from 6 to
19. Seventy-five per cent were between the ages of
9.5 and 16.5. The investigators state that because of the
care in selection of the subjects they "feel justified in in-
ferring that the experimental children represent a fair sampling of an average child population and that the regularity
of the conditions of living at the Bureau favors rather than
calls into question the general applicability of the conclusions" based upon their experimental results.

The apparatus was interesting. Children were studied
in groups of ten boys and of ten girls. Beneath the single
bed of each child was attached a hypnograph unit which
caused an electrical contact to break whenever the occu-
pant of the bed moved slightly. The hypnograph was connected by wire with a polygraph unit which on rolls of
paper provided records of the periods of quiescence and
motility of each child.

In all 163 children were used. Records were kept for 347
nights in nine experiments. This produced a total of 6,650
child nights of sleep—equivalent in mere amount to 18
years of study of one child.

The first step in each experiment was to establish a
stable sleep pattern for each hour of the night for each
child. The investigators found that the hourly motility
distribution is a characteristic that is stable to a high degree
under normal routine living undisturbed by illness, emotional upsets, etc. Incidentally the average child aged 6 to
18 stirs or rearranges his position once each 8.7 minutes.

The normal sleep pattern having been established for

each subject at the beginning of each experiment, the children left the Bureau at 6:20 P.M.; were taken on foot in orderly fashion to a neighborhood theater; returned by 8:45; and were in bed promptly at 9:00. In all they saw 58 pictures which happened to be showing on the nights they attended.

The experiments exhibited a variety of forms. For instance one series consisted of ten normal nights, ten movie nights, and five normal nights. Another distribution was: fourteen normal nights, six movies in two weeks to approximate the distribution and frequency of attendance of many average children, and eight normal nights.

Children were also taken on interesting trips, as a substitute for movie going, to check against the hypothesis that measurable results of movie attendance may be due to a "holiday effect." The influence of humidity and temperature on sleep patterns was investigated. And as has been indicated the children were on certain controlled occasions provided with coffee and Kaffee Hag at the evening meal and at 8:30 P.M. They were on occasion kept up until 12:00 at night and again asked to rise three hours earlier in the morning than usual to compare the resulting sleep patterns with those that followed movie attendance. (The children considered all these experiments as thrilling adventures for which they felt they were fortunate to be selected.)

For our purposes three significant findings stand out in these studies.

First, increase in motility following the movies ranged from 0 to 90 per cent. On the average boys showed 26 per cent and girls 14 per cent greater hourly motility after movies than in normal sleep. Twenty-five per cent increase is equivalent approximately to pushing an 8 year old boy until he is as restless in sleep as a 12 year old normally is. The boys and girls are more restless than they normally should be. To these increases are to be added cases of children who show symptoms of fatigue in the form of decreased motility which according to the scientific literature is equally important as a measure of fatigue. The effect of movie attendance is measured by deviations from normal sleep in both directions—increased and decreased motility.

Second, 50 per cent of the boys show half as much or more change from the normal after seeing all types of movies as they show following enforced sitting up for three additional hours from 9:00 to midnight. On the average, a boy who went to the movies and was in bed by nine in the evening was as restless in sleep as if he had sat up until midnight before going to bed. Many individuals showed even greater change after certain impressive pictures. Movie influence was persistent beyond the movie night and was dependent upon the age, sex, and mental "set" of the child. Continued sleep deprivation in the mornings or evenings produced disciplinary conditions so serious that the matrons asked that the sleep deprivation experiments be discontinued. Matinee attendance would probably show as great an effect as night attendance or even greater.

These facts indicate the conclusion that parents who allow their children to go to a movie should do so with the knowledge that the experience is about as disturbing to sleep patterns as sitting up till midnight or that the influence of some pictures on motility is as great on some children as the drinking of two cups of coffee in the evening.

Third, numerous variations in the effects of the movies to modify the averages were observed by the investigators. Notably some pictures are much more disturbing to sleep patterns than others. Equally significant, some children are much more affected by some pictures than are other children. In general the sleep motility of children below ten is affected less by attendance from 6:30 to 8:30 in the evening than is that of older children. But again there are exceptions and variations.

The investigators summarize: "We can conclude, however, from our results that seeing *some* films does induce a disturbance of relaxed, recuperative sleep in children to a degree which, if indulged in with sufficient frequency, can be regarded as detrimental to normal health and growth. We do not believe that any sweeping generalizations can be made about the 'type' of film or 'type' of child most likely to be influenced. There is a distinct need for careful intensive study on individual children's reactions to movies."

Thus it appears that movies selected unwisely and indulged in intemperately will have a detrimental effect upon the health of children. This is the fourth link in the chain of evidence.

INFLUENCING CONDUCT

CONDUCT is a product of many factors. Of these factors the preceding investigations have explored four. We may assume the obvious position that information is a factor in behavior: what one knows determines in part what one does. We may also assume that attitudes toward social objects affect conduct: if one is friendly toward an objective of action in a situation he will be influenced to build one behavior pattern; if unfriendly, to build another. It may also be fairly assumed that experiences which are accompanied by excitement and emotion have a more powerful effect upon conduct than do those which are placid and uninteresting. Likewise, we may assume that fatigue expressed either by increased or decreased sleep motility results in producing a tone of behavior by which conduct patterns are affected. We have seen that motion pictures have an influence upon all of these factors.

We were able to check the validity of these assumptions, which square with common sense, by a mass of evidence from the studies of Blumer and his associates. Here it was possible to secure hundreds of cases in which the information and attitudes acquired in the movies were directly operative in the conduct of children.

Blumer, Thrasher, and their associates [9] supplemented the foregoing indirect studies of conduct by investigating the direct relationships existing between movies and conduct. Blumer used an autobiography technique, supplemented by interviews, accounts of conversations, and questionnaires. His major study was based upon the case reports of 634 students in two universities, 481 college and junior-college students in four colleges, 583 high-school students, 67 office workers, and 58 factory workers. After studying many biographies written without specific directions and discovering the patterns into which they unconsciously fell, he formulated a few questions to guide the writers as follows: trace the history of your interest in the movies; describe how motion pictures have affected your emotions and your moods; write fully about what you have imitated from the movies; describe your experience with pictures of love and romance; write fully about any ambitions and temptations you have gotten from the movies. Unusual care was taken to preserve the anonymity of the writers. Interviews were held with 81 university students who had previously written autobiographies and 54 high-school students who had not. Careful accounts of con-

[9] *Movies and Conduct*, by Herbert Blumer; *Movies, Delinquency, and Crime*, by Herbert Blumer and Philip M. Hauser; *Boys, Movies, and City Streets*, by Paul G. Cressey and Frederick M. Thrasher.

versations were secured from several fraternities, several sororities, and girls' groups and from several cliques of high-school boys and girls, from conversations of high-school boys and girls at parties, and from boys' gangs, play groups, office girls, and factory workers. Direct questionnaires were administered to 1,200 children in the fifth and sixth grades of 12 public schools in Chicago distributed between schools in high, medium, and low delinquency areas. One set of questionnaires was filled out by a special school for truants and boys with behavior problems. Direct observations were made of children while in attendance at small neighborhood theaters.

From these sources a huge mass of materials was collected. The materials were analyzed to discover trends and significant facts. The main use of the material "has been to show and illuminate the different kinds of ways in which motion pictures touch the lives of young people." Experiences which recurred with a high rate of frequency in the separate documents were selected and samples of each type were presented in the report.

Obviously the validity of personal reports is an issue that has a bearing upon the conclusions of the investigators. Upon this question Blumer took all known precautions against error and presents the following facts about the safeguards which they threw around the investigations: (1) Machinery was set up to demonstrate in an obvious manner the anonymity of the written accounts. (2) The utmost care and attention were devoted to gaining full coöperation from the students in securing their frank, honest, and unexaggerated statements. (3) The interviews held six months after the autobiographies were written were used in the cases of some 60 students with their consent but without this previous knowledge as a check against agreement between the content of the written report and the substance of the interview; no discrepancy of importance was discovered. (4) The accounts were checked for internal consistency and some twenty which showed contradiction were discarded. (5) Conversations were checked against the written reports. (6) Individuals were asked to write only about those experiences which they recalled vividly.

The chief means of checking the character of the experiences given in the written documents was "in the comparison of document with document. The accounts were written independently by students in different schools and localities. . . . The comparison of large numbers of documents coming from different groups of people with no knowledge of each other made it possible to ascertain the general run of experiences. The contents of documents coming from different sources yielded substantially the same general kind of experiences."

In short the validity of the report is determined by the care taken to secure valid materials and by the mass and consistency of testimony bearing upon significant issues. This mass and consistency protects the validity of the conclusions.

Foremost among the contributions of these reports is the elaboration of the phenomenon of "emotional possession" which is characteristic of the experience of children before the motion-picture screen. Watching in the dark of the theater, the young child sits in the presence of reality when he observes the actors perform and the plot of the drama unfold. He sees the actions of people living in a real world— not of actors playing a make-believe rôle. His emotions are aroused in ways that have been described. He forgets his surroundings. He loses ordinary control of his feelings, his actions, and his thoughts. He identifies himself with the plot and loses himself in the picture. His "emotional condition may get such a strong grip on him that even his efforts to rid himself of it by reasoning with himself may prove of little avail." He is possessed by the drama.

The intensity of child experience in viewing pictures cannot be fully appreciated by adults. To adults the picture is good or bad, the acting satisfactory or unsatisfactory, the singing up to or not up to standard. To them a picture is just a picture. They may recall memories of thrills they used to have but the memories are pale in comparison to the actual experience. They get a more vivid impression of this excitement by watching a theater full of children as a thrilling drama unreels. They see the symptoms of keen emotion. But even in the presence of these manifestations they miss the depth and intensity of the child's experience.

Several factors contribute to emotional possession. The actions and the setting are concrete. When in the fairy story the child is told that the prince led his troops into battle he has to provide his own imagery; but in the picture he sees the charming prince at the head of a band of "real" men. Every significant visual image is provided before his eyes in the motion picture. He does not have to translate the words in which the story is conveyed. He sees machines; he does not hear about them. He visits the islands of the southern seas in a real ship; he does not have to listen to a narrator describe the scenes in words alone. The motion picture tells a very concrete and simple tale in a fashion which makes the story easy to grasp.

Emotional possession is also caused by the dramatic forms of the picture. One of the objectives of drama is to arouse the emotions. Indeed, the weakness of many "teaching films" is the absence of dramatic elements—often necessarily omitted because of the nature of the content to be taught. But in the commercial movies and in teaching films of action, the dramatic flow of the story stirs the emotions and produces that intensity of experience which Blumer calls "emotional possession."

A third factor which contributes its influence to this condition is the attractiveness of the pictures—beautiful and thrilling scenes, interesting people, attractive persons moving on the stage, stimulating colors, expert lighting, and the like. The child wants to be a part of such a bit of life. He does not pull back from the experience; he hurls himself into it.

All of these factors and probably others produce a condition that is favorable to certain types of learning. This is the quality of authority. Children accept as true, correct, proper, right what they see on the screen. They have little knowledge. The people on the screen are confidence-producing. Everything works to build up a magnificent and impressive world. Holaday and Stoddard found the children accepting both fact and error as fact. Blumer indicates the power of movie patterns upon conduct. The authority of the screen may account for some of the striking change of attitude of children found by Peterson and Thurstone.

All of these considerations lead inevitably to the increasing strength of the conclusion that the motion picture is an extremely powerful medium of education.

A second conclusion drawn from the report is that the range of influence of movies is very wide. Blumer found in studying two thousand children what every parent knows about his own child—that the movies dominate the patterns of play of children in a wide variety of forms. He presents scores of cases to show that the world of phantasy of young children and adolescents and of both sexes is ruled by movie subjects. Dozens of cases are presented to show the effects of the movies in stimulating emotions of fright, sorrow, love, and "excitement." Cases are presented to illustrate how the movies give children techniques of action in situations which are of interest to them ranging from the trivial techniques of the playground to disturbing cues for the delinquent. And most far-reaching of all he indicates how they stir powerful ambitions, good and bad; develop permanent ideals, high and low; and crystallize the framework of life careers. In most unexpected quarters the influence of the movies is discovered in the reports of Blumer and Thrasher and their associates.

A third concept which supplements emotional possession and range of influence is the guidance concept which grows out of the preceding paragraph. Children are born into a world of which they know nothing. They are little individualists who have laboriously to learn how to fit into social groups. They possess impulses, instincts, wishes, desires, which drive them on to seek experience, adventure, and satisfaction. They are avidly interested in everything that seems to them to be able to provide what they want.

Yet they know so little and are so anxious to learn. They seek information, stimulation, and guidance in every direction. They are often confused, frequently maladjusted, and sometimes without confidence. In this situation the motion picture seems to be a godsend to them. While they are being entertained they are being shown in attractive and authoritative fashion what to do. They are guided in one direction or another as they absorb rightly or wrongly this idea or that one. Sometimes the guidance is good, at other times it is bad. Sometimes it lies in a direction opposed to the teachings of the home or the school; at other times it reinforces them. But always the motion picture is potentially a powerfully influential director. Not the only guide which leads them, to be sure: the community, chums and playmates, the home, the school, the church, the newspapers, all are used by these omnivorous seekers after the kinds of experience they want. But among them the motion picture possesses potency so substantial that society must not fail to understand and see that it is used beneficently in the guidance of children.

One means of helping the child to dominate his movie experiences rather than be possessed emotionally by them is a fourth product of these investigations. It is possible to increase control of movie experiences by developing what Ruckmick calls adult discount and Blumer describes as emotional detachment. Blumer describes one interesting series of cases to show the stages of growth of this maturer attitude. Certain fourth graders showed in the most undisguised fashion a great interest in serial thrillers and particularly in one. They talked freely and spoke with frank enthusiasm. The sixth graders were reluctant to talk. They admitted interest yet felt some shame at their interest in a "childish" picture. Their attitude was one of affected sophistication. The attitude of the eighth graders was, however, one of spontaneous and frank disapproval, dislike, and disgust at serials. The steps were three in number, frank approval, affected sophistication, and mature disapproval.

Three methods of developing adult discount or emotional detachment are mentioned by Blumer. The one most commonly present in the evolution of children's attitudes is the response to the attitude of slightly older groups or the "sophisticated" members of one's own group—as just indicated. The child is quick to put away childish things when his group frowns upon them as childish and he enjoys exhibiting superiority and sophistication. In later years and with wider experience adult discount may be produced by a second factor: the conviction that the pictures are not true to life. "In real life things aren't that way." This is a normal method of developing sophistication. The third method is to give children instruction about the movies. Sometimes Blumer found that talks with parents, or suggestions that "this is only make believe" from older people, helped the children to develop emotional detachment. Particularly, however, detachment comes with learning how pictures are made, how effects are secured, what to look for in pictures, what makes pictures artistically good or bad. Dale's appreciation study contributes to this end.

In summary of the direct influences of motion pictures on conduct: they owe their power over children chiefly to the factor of emotional possession; the range of influence of commercial movies is very wide; the motion picture because of its potency in many directions plays a substantial and significant rôle in the informal guidance of children; and the influence of pictures can be controlled in considerable measure by the development of emotional detachment and the application of an adult discount. In producing this intelligent attitude toward the movies, instruction in motion-picture criticism and appreciation provides a promising lead.

With this section, we have concluded a description of the studies which essayed to measure the influence of the motion picture as such. We see that as an instrument of education it has unusual power to impart information, to influence specific attitudes toward objects of social value, to affect emotions either in gross or in microscopic proportions, to affect health in a minor degree through sleep disturbance, and to affect profoundly the patterns of conduct of children.

It is now appropriate to examine the content of current

movies and discover the directions in which they are probably leading attitudes and conduct.

ATTENDING THE MOVIES

IN calculating the effect of commercial movies upon children it is necessary to know the extent to which children are exposed to them. This information was collected by Dale [10] in two forms: the attendance of children per week and the percentage of children found in audiences.

The attendance per week was estimated by studying the reports of 55,000 children from the kindergarten through the twelfth grade in 44 representative communities in Ohio and three communities outside the state. His study was checked against 18 other studies previously made (but none so large nor so carefully conducted) and all were found to give slightly larger numbers than his.

The attendance data were gathered directly from school children above the third grade on printed blanks and from younger children by interviews. The validity of the information so obtained was checked by three techniques and found to be satisfactory.

The children were asked to state how often they attended the movies during the preceding seven days and the weeks were scattered throughout the school year. Dale found that among children from 5 to 8 the average attendance per week was .42 times and that 22 per cent never attend. The average boy of age 5 to 8 attends 24 picture programs a year and the average girl 19. In the age range 8 to 19 the average attendance was .99 or approximately once a week and only 5 per cent never attend. The average boy in this range attends 57 picture programs a year and the average girl 46 in the same period.

[10] *Children's Attendance at Motion Pictures*, by Edgar Dale.

Children above 7 years of age on the average attend the movies once a week. In the age range 8 to 19, 27 per cent of the boys and 21 per cent of the girls attend twice or more. Children in rural areas attend less frequently than urban children.

It was found that fathers take their boys of ages 8 to 19 very infrequently—2.63 per cent of all cases. Mothers accompany their sons about 3.65 per cent of the times and this percentage drops almost consistently from attendance with 8 year olds to 19 year olds. Boys of 8 are accompanied by both parents 23 per cent of the times they attend. Brothers or sisters accompany each other to the movies in 14.81 per cent of the cases. The percentage of brother-sister attendance remains stationary from 8 to 11 years at about 22 per cent and drops steadily to 4.43 per cent at 18. Going with some one else averages 11.45 per cent. It steadily rises from 8 to 17 years of age with a plateau thereafter. Going by one's self remains fairly constant around an average of 25 per cent, except for the 8 and 9 year olds, who go alone less often.

Fathers go with girls on exactly the same percentage of occasions as they go with boys. Mothers attend nearly three times as often with daughters as with sons and with 8 year old daughters one third of the times they go. The percentage falls for mothers consistently thereafter. In girls' attendance with own friends the curves closely resemble the boys'. With "some one else" they go more frequently and by themselves only one third as often as the boys. The order of frequency for boys from frequent to infrequent is: own friends, alone, brother or sister, some one else, both parents, mother, and father. For girls it runs: own friends, brother or sister, some one else, mother, alone, and father.

About 80 per cent of the boys and girls stay in the theater for only one showing. About 18 per cent of boys and girls see the feature through twice. About 20 per cent of the boys see the news reel through twice and 26 per cent the comedy twice. The girls stay somewhat less often for these. One per cent of boys and girls stay three times for feature, news reel, and comedy. Only 2 per cent of the girls reporting attend the theaters in the mornings. In the afternoons 33 per cent are found in attendance. From the age of 13 to 19 the percentages drop from 38 to 14. In the evenings the average attendance for girls is 64 per cent. To the age of 13 the percentages of evening attendance cluster around 55. Thereafter they rise slowly to 84 for the 19 year olds. The boys' figures are approximately the same.

In general for children of both sexes the attendance in the morning is negligible, in the afternoon about one third; in the evenings two thirds of the children's attendance is found. The most popular days of the week are Saturday, 34 per cent, Sunday, 27 per cent, and Friday, 12 per cent. The average of the other days of the week is approximately 7 per cent.

The proportion of children in the theater audience was based upon the Columbus study. Attendance was clocked at 15 representative theaters out of a total of 43 theaters in the city. The audience entering was classified by trained observers into four age groups: under 7, 8 to 13, 14 to 20, and 21 and over. The study was scattered over approximately three months with about 240,000 persons in attendance per week.

It was found that 3.1 per cent of those entering the theaters were under seven years of age; 7 to 13 years of age, 13.7 per cent; 14 to 20 years, 20.8 per cent; and 21 or over, 62.4 per cent. Thus approximately 17 per cent of the audiences were grade-school children and 37 per cent were minors. The percentage of children under 14 years found in audiences in different types of theater ran as follows: good neighborhood, 27.9; poor neighborhood, 23.3; good all-Negro, 14.7; poor downtown, 8.0; and good downtown, 5.5. It is of interest to note that at all ages there were more males than females in the audiences. At ages 7 to 13 the proportion of boys to girls was 64 to 36; at ages 14 to 20, 57 to 43; and above 20, 59 to 41.

Calculations based upon these studies and other data led Dale to the conclusion that there were in weekly attendance at theaters throughout the nation 11,000,000 children under 14 years of age and 28,000,000 minors.

From this study of attendance it can be conservatively concluded that 11,000,000 children attend motion pictures once a week, that 17 per cent of the audiences are made up of children under 14 years of age, and that 37 per cent are minors. Obviously, whether or not these figures are exact within a million or so, it may be concluded if one notes the age spread of attendance that children are exposed to all the films that are shown in commercial theaters.

The content of the pictures thus becomes a matter of deep concern to parents. If the commercial movies reinforce the training of the home, the school, and the church, parents have cause for deep satisfaction. If they conflict with the teachings of these agencies parents who believe in the teachings of the home, the school, and the church will be seriously disturbed. Light is thrown upon this critical question by the studies of Dale, Peters, Blumer, Thrasher, and their associates.

THE CONTENT OF CURRENT MOVIES

THE influences of commercial movies are felt in many directions. They provide entertainment in agreeable theater surroundings for millions of people. They display beautiful scenes from all parts of the world. The action of the drama is rapid and often thrilling. Movies have a marked effect upon wearing apparel and social manners. They provide romance for millions who feel little of romance in their daily lives.

These contributions of the commercial movies are fully recognized by thoughtful people. Our investigations, however, concerned themselves only incidentally with phases of the motion picture that did not directly influence the attitudes and conduct of children. No attention in a major degree was paid to their effects upon adults, which is quite another problem to be solved in the light of many considerations which are not germane to the problem of influence upon children. Theoretically the commercial movies might be quite unobjectionable for seasoned adults and still be quite unsuitable for children. Adults are mature and accepted judges of what they choose to see. But toward children American society has taken a protective attitude. Knowing that children are immature, society is convinced that the experiences to which they are exposed should be selected to produce beneficial results upon character and conduct. American society is deeply concerned about the moral influences which surround its young.

Turning to the content of commercial pictures and viewing it against this background, we find that Dale [11] analyzed the themes of 500 feature pictures shown in each of the years 1920, 1925, and 1930 with the aid of the Harrison Reports. In conducting his analysis he discovered 10 classes of theme: crime, sex, love, comedy, mystery, war, children (about children or for children), history, travel, and social propaganda. The pictures were classified by individual readers. The judgment of each reader

[11] *The Content of Motion Pictures*, by Edgar Dale.

was checked in samplings of 100 pictures shown in each of the three years by having three readers classify each of the 300 pictures. The three readers agreed in nine out of ten cases, which was sufficiently close agreement to establish approximate reliability of the judgment of each reader. When there was more than one theme in a picture it was allocated to the class to which the major theme belonged.

The Big Three among the themes in 1930 were: love 29.6 per cent, crime 27.4 per cent, and sex 15.0 per cent, making a total of 72 per cent of all themes. That is, in 1930 approximately 7 out of 10 pictures exhibited one of the Big Three as their major themes. The percentages of themes in 1920, 1925, and 1930 were substantially the same except for the theme of love. The love percentages in 1920, 1925, and 1930 were respectively the following: 44.6, 32.8, and 29.6. For crime pictures the following percentages occurred in the same years: 24.0, 29.6, and 27.4; and for sex: 13.0, 16.8, and 15.0. Comedy aggregating 16 per cent in 1930 and mystery and war, together totaling 8.6 per cent, followed the Big Three. The other four classes divided the remaining pictures, 3.4 per cent, among them: out of 500 pictures in 1930 one was a children's picture, seven were historical films, nine were travel pictures, and no social-propaganda picture was included.

An analysis of the Big Three was conducted by the investigator. Under the 27.4 per cent of crime pictures was included those dealing in a major way with: blackmailing; extortion; injury, hate, and revenge—the idea of vengeance— feuds; corruption in politics or business, bribery, swindling, crook plays, criminal activity predominant; racketeers, bootleggers, gamblers, gangsters, smugglers, thieves; outlaws, bandits, rustlers—"western" type—holdups, gun fighting, etc., being the main interest; and criminal types and activities—prison stories. When one goes to the movies once a week he sees on the average one such picture a little oftener than once a month.

The criminals are not frequently starred as attractive characters. In almost two thirds of the cases adults classify them as unattractive; how children classify them was not discovered. Dale says, "It is evident, however, that movie criminals are not always shown as low, cowardly, weak-minded, and physically repulsive. The evidence strongly suggests that no small proportion of the criminals are accomplished in some of the social graces and many are well-dressed. Not infrequently we see on the screen criminals who are courageous and meet danger fearlessly."

When the pictures present the solution for the crime problem presented in a picture the investigator says, "The fundamental philosophy of movie criminology is that the crimes are committed by bad people. Therefore, jail or deport the criminals and the crime problem is solved."

In 115 pictures selected at random in 1932 as they appeared in the theaters of Columbus, Ohio, some interesting details were analyzed. Fifty-nine of the 115 pictures showed killing techniques of a wide variety. This is at the rate of approximately one in every other picture. In 45, killings occurred, and in 21, killings were attempted. The revolver was used in 22 pictures, knifing in 9, general shooting in 5. In less than 5 pictures each were shown: hanging, stabbing, beating to death, drowning, lynching, machine-gunning, strangling, and eight other methods, making a total of 18 varieties of exits from the movie scenes of action.

Out of 115 pictures analyzed and the 59 pictures of these in which killings occurred or were attempted, the heroine slipped three times in attempts to kill and got her man only once. Heroines in movie tradition, like kings in chess, are to be protected. The heroes, however, were in 14 tight places where lethal weapons were needed, and they did much better jobs than the heroines. They were successful in 13 out of 14 tries. The villains came oftener to bat than the heroes, but with a lower batting average. They made only 22 hits out of 42 times at bat, with a percentage of .524—the heroes' percentage was .929. The lady villains were responsible for 8 murders. The rest of the carnage was contributed by other men and women in the casts.

This is a rather sorry layout for the children to see when they go to the movies. One out of four of all the films are crime pictures and crimes are committed in many more than those in which they are the central theme.

Pictures of sex constitute 15 per cent of the 500 pictures studied for 1930. In this class are listed pictures whose major themes are: living together without marriage being apparent; loose living, impropriety known or implied; plot revolving around seduction, adultery, kept women, illegitimate children the central characters, sex situations; "women for sale" stuff; bedroom farce with incidents on the fringes of sexual impropriety. Among the 115 pictures analyzed in detail, 22 (or one out of five) presented illicit love as a goal of 35 leading characters: the heroes (4); the heroines (3); the villains (11) the villainesses (7); and other men and women (10).

Romantic love pictures (29.6 per cent in 1930) include in the class: love against a background of thrills, suspense, or melodrama; courtship, love, flirtations, marital difficulties; historical romance; operetta type, colorful scenes and songs. Some of these are beautiful and in good taste, others are sensual and in conflict with the mores of every group studied by Peters. Blumer has shown how techniques of love-making are learned by the adolescents. He and Ruckmick have shown the intense emotional possession experienced by the 16 year olds. They eat them up, and 3 out of 10 pictures present the major theme of love. The 72 per cent devoted to the Big Three produce an unbalanced diet for the children to digest. Occasional pictures of these sorts can be vigorously defended. But 7 out of 10 provide a diet too narrow for the welfare of children.

The goals attempted by the characters throw further light on the content of the pictures. Here the investigator sought in 115 pictures to classify the goals of the leading characters. In all 883 goals were detected. Winning another's love constituted 18 per cent; and marriage for love, 8 per cent; illicit love, 4 per cent; conquering a rival, 2 per cent; protection of loved one, 2 per cent—a total of 34 per cent goals of love. The range extended to other goals— professional success, revenge, crime for gain, performance of duty, financial success, and a very large class of goals not easy to classify constituting 29 per cent of the total.

A number of analyses of specific details are relevant to the question. Of these one is selected. Dale found that in the 115 pictures analyzed, 90, or 78 per cent, or four out of five, contained liquor situations. In 49 of the 115, or in 43 per cent, intoxication was shown. In 43 per cent of the cases the hero drank and in 23 per cent the heroine imbibed. The villains and the "lady" villains together only slightly surpassed the heroines, and did not equal the wetness of the heroes. Generally speaking, one can safely conclude that the commercial movies are dripping wet.

To the Dale studies which established the central trends of the commercial movies of 1920 to 1932 may be added the analyses of 142 pictures made by Peters and his associates. They conducted in their study of movies and mores [12] four

[12] *Motion Pictures and Standards of Morality*, by Charles C. Peters.

interesting analyses of details of pictures which appeared in the local theaters. In 142 pictures they found 726 scenes depicting aggressiveness of girls in love-making; of these actions 549 were performed by attractive characters and 177 by unattractive persons. They found also in the 142 pictures, 741 scenes of kissing and caressing mostly by casual lovers (383); partly by betrothed lovers (200), and partly by married persons (157). They analyzed the 142 pictures for democractic attitudes and practices and found 303 scenes depicting the treatment of employees and subordinates, 250 scenes in which social "superiors" dealt with social "inferiors," and 60 scenes in which racial discrimination was present. In the same pictures they observed and rated 522 scenes depicting the treatment of children by parents— 97 involving the discipline of children, 347 involving companionship with children, and 78 depicting self-sacrifice of parents for children. The quality of these scenes will be described later.

Movies and Conduct and *Movies, Delinquency, and Crime* present by implication an additional mass of information about the content of commercial pictures. One can deduce the content of pictures by watching the play of children and noting their phantasy life. Dress and manners of the characters are noted and imitated. Techniques of love-making are found and copied. Fear pictures, sentimental pictures, and exciting films abound and exert their influence. Strivings for ambitious ends are presented and arouse ambitions in a variety of directions. The freedom of youth and the adventurous lives of the characters are represented and may cause discontent with homes and neighborhoods to arise. Some plays portray family affection and loyalty and to these many children respond successfully.

Crime pictures have a pronounced effect upon delinquents. Minor delinquencies are aggravated by these pictures in many cases; cues for criminal actions are presented
and are sometimes copied by young delinquents. The
"easy money" and the luxury shown in the movies leave
traces in the memories and conduct of delinquents. Criminal-
action pictures make some youths "want to fight" because
of emotional possession. "You get a lot of thrill out of them."
Crime pictures aggravate daydreaming about lives of
crime. Techniques of crime are numerous in pictures and
concretely portrayed. Blumer and Hauser collected from
their materials a large number of techniques that had been
noted and sometimes used by delinquents: how to open a
safe by the feel of the dial, how to act and what to do in
robbery with a gun, how to jimmy a window, how to force
an automobile door with a piece of pipe, how to take doors
off hinges in burglarizing a house, eluding police in the dark,
how to pick pockets, the use of ether in burglarizing, putting burglar alarms out of commission, and so on and so on.
To be sure, the delinquent might have learned these techniques without the movies. We had delinquency before
commercial motion pictures were invented. But crime
movies are handy and it is easy to learn from them if one is
interested in delinquent behavior. One's education in crime
advances more rapidly by means of crime pictures.

The sex pictures have an extremely powerful influence
upon many delinquents. Sexual passions are aroused and
amateur prostitution is aggravated. The fast life depicted
by the movie characters on the screen induces desires, they
say, for such a life. Luxury and smart appearance make
an enormous appeal, particularly to many female delinquents. Granted that reports from delinquents are not
completely reliable, the fact still remains that enough of

them can quote chapter and verse to show that crime and sex pictures are at least an aggravating influence in their conduct.

From all these data collected about the content of pictures the conclusion is inevitable that from the point of view of children's welfare the commercial movies are an unsavory mess. For adults the selection of movies is their own business, to be controlled by whatever means they want to use. But children have crashed the gate in millions—eager-minded, ripe for learning; and three weeks out of four on their once-a-week trips to the movies they see a crime picture, a love picture, and a sex picture. The producers ought to have a heart.

Peters [13] devised a technique for judging whether pictures were morally "good" or "bad." The technique perfected was quite ingenious. He assumes that pictures are good if they are congruent with the mores, beliefs, or conventions and are bad if they are in conflict with them. This means that goodness or badness is based upon the sensibilities of the people concerned. These sensibilities by which groups come to feel that certain acts are "bad" and others "good" are the product of long experience and are more than likely to be correct for their time and place. These group feelings come to be accepted by the individuals who make up the group, so that one can get evidence of the attitude of the group as a whole from the reaction of a comparatively few of its members. In this sense, then, the "morality" of motion pictures may be gauged by securing the response of a comparatively small number of "judges" who because they have assimilated the point of view of their group, can speak for the group. But in most communities there are several groups and consequently

[13] *Motion Pictures and Standards of Morality*, by Charles C. Peters.

several "public opinions" about moral questions, so that parents, for instance, who seek for good pictures for their children must either see them themselves or trust the judgment of some person or group whose tastes and beliefs they believe to be like their own.

Relying upon this definition of morality Peters proceeded to study four types of scenes in pictures: aggressiveness of a girl in love-making, kissing and caressing, democratic attitudes and practices, and the treatment of children by parents.

The method used was the same in each case. He first constructed a scale of incidents in each area. This was done by collecting a large number of incidents related to each— and then asking each of several groups of persons to rate the incidents as "admired," disapproved, or neutral. Upon this basis by the use of statistical procedures he was able to rank the incidents from the extremes of approval to the opposite extreme of disapproval. In carrying out the procedure he was able to secure quantities to express the attitude of such groups as college professors, young miners, ministers, factory girls, "society girls," and the like. Incidentally, the college professors and their wives were the most conservative of all the groups on the issues studied. In the scale for aggressive love-making the order of the groups ranked from conservativeness to liberality were: faculty, adult Brethren, preachers of the United States, college senior boys, college senior girls, young Brethren, Junior League girls, Hampton Institute Negroes, graduate students, members of the Motion Picture Research Council, business men, factory workers, adult miners, and young miners. The position of the Research Council members among the least conservative groups is of passing interest.

When the scales were perfected five observers were

trained to analyze each of 142 pictures in the theater and
to place the scenes in their appropriate places on the scale.
The composite judgment of the five observers was calcu-
lated for each scene and the positions of the scenes were
compared with the judgments of the groups whose positions upon the scales had been determined as indicated.

In the 142 pictures 522 scenes depicting the treatment of
children by parents were observed. Of these 445 were scenes
in which the parents were attractive characters and 77
were unattractive. In these scenes the conduct of parents
in the movies was above the average of the groups from the
standpoint of whose moral codes the scales were made. If
one sets the approval of the upper 25 per cent of each group
as a high standard of excellence, 41 per cent of the scenes
were satisfactory. Seventy per cent of all the scenes were
satisfactory to the average of the groups. Thus on the whole
the treatment of children tends in an upward rather than
a downward direction. On the average children are treated
better in the movies than they are treated outside.

In the 142 pictures 741 kissing and caressing scenes were
studied. Of these Peters says "the conduct in motion pictures, as far as kissing is concerned, is closely parallel to
that of life in the six social groups studied so far as the conduct of attractive characters is concerned but the conduct
in motion pictures is worse than life when we consider both
attractive and unattractive characters."

In the study of democratic attitudes 303 scenes were observed in which the treatment of employees, "inferior"
races, and persons of "inferior" social standing were rated.
Here "the findings indicate that motion pictures stand
rather above the mores in respect to democratic attitudes
and practices."

In aggressiveness of a girl in love-making the case is less

favorable. In 726 scenes studied, of which 549 were played by attractive characters, it was found that only 12 per cent of the scenes were such as half the combined groups would admire and 56 per cent of the scenes would be actively disapproved by half the groups. Eighty-five per cent would be disapproved by the upper quarter of the groups. Among the groups 95 per cent of the scenes would be disapproved by the upper 25 per cent of strict adult Brethren; but 64 per cent were disapproved even by the upper quarter of adolescent miners—the most liberal. And 25 per cent of the scenes would be disapproved by three quarters of the young miners. When Peters studied the relation of practice in this area with approved standards he found that practice was also below the approved level and that motion-picture conduct in aggressiveness of girls was about on a level with practice. "It is clear," writes Peters, "that motion pictures are bucking hard against present standards of value in relation to aggressiveness in love-making. Practice, too, seems to be taking the reins but against a certain feeling of propriety yet persisting. It is clear that the mores (in the sense of *approved* customs) cannot long lag behind practice; especially when the suggestions of skillfully constructed drama tend constantly to give sanction to the deviating patterns and thus win approval for them."

The major points of interest in this study are two in number. First Peters has clearly defined good and bad. They are determined by the approval of judges. A picture is good if congruent with the mores and bad if in conflict with them. This holds for the mores of individuals or of groups. And as has been remarked above, the practical procedures for a parent in selecting pictures for children to see if he cannot pre-view them himself is to take the opinion of individuals or groups whose taste he believes to be like his own. Second, some scenes in the movies are admired, others merit disapproval of all Peters' groups. But in the matter of aggressive love-making by girls the conduct depicted in the movies is distinctly below the approved standards of every group studied.

TEACHING DISCRIMINATION TO CHILDREN

IN conclusion the investigators attacked the control of motion-picture influence in one direction. They concluded that they could experiment with one constructive safeguard against bad movies and one aid to good movies. Dale [14] accordingly prepared a textbook for high-school boys and girls on motion-picture appreciation and criticism. The intent was to teach the adolescent how to judge pictures for himself by setting standards, and to teach him how to apply them. It was believed that a discriminating audience would be a constructive power for control of what would be produced.

The techniques of assembling the materials were simple because motion pictures are a form of art and drama. In these fields the underlying principles have already been worked out and used in the high-school study of art appreciation and literature including the drama. These were assembled from authoritative sources and applied to the photoplay. In making the applications the assistance of experts in the appropriate fields was secured. When the materials were assembled they were tried out experimentally in selected schools in 1931 to 1932. During 1932 to 1933 the materials are being revised again in connection with the teaching of motion-picture appreciation over the radio broadcast to high-school students and adult discussion groups. It is also being used on a wider scale in high schools

[14] *How to Appreciate Motion Pictures*, by Edgar Dale.

than in the previous year. Particularly fruitful contacts were made with the Photoplay Committee of the National Council of Teachers of English. This contact is valuable because the normal avenue of approach to the teaching of motion-picture appreciation in the high school is through teachers of courses in English and because the Committee of the Council has been vigorously promoting motion-picture appreciation for two or three years. The experimental program of the committee is meeting with success in utilizing the unusual interest of high-school students in motion pictures, and promises to be a constructive measure in teaching adolescents how to discriminate among motion pictures—to help them to enjoy good art and drama more deeply and criticize bad pictures more intelligently.

CONCLUSION

As one reviews the series of studies three conclusions seem inevitable. First, the motion picture, as such, is a potent medium of education. Children even of the early age of 8 see half the facts in a picture and remember them for a surprisingly long time. A single exposure to a picture may produce a measurable change in attitude. Emotions are measurably stirred as the scenes of a drama unfold and this excitement may be recorded in deviations from the norm in sleep patterns, by visible gross evidences of bodily movement and by refined internal responses. They constitute patterns of conduct in daydreaming, phantasy, and action. The evidence of their influence is massive and irrefutable.

Second, for children the content of current pictures is not good. There is too much sex and crime and love for a balanced diet for children. These impartial studies reveal much more harm than help. Stoddard, Thurstone, Ruckmick, Blumer, and their associates indicate the power of the motion picture. But Dale, Blumer, Thrasher, Peters, and their associates clearly indicate that the power flows too much in dangerous directions.

Third, the motion-picture situation is very complicated. It is one among many influences which mold the experience of children. How powerful this is in relation to the influence of the ideals taught in the home, in the school, and in the church by street life and companions or by community customs, these studies have not canvassed. May and Shuttleworth found in their survey study that in attitude toward the great majority of specific objects examined there was little difference between those children who go often to the movies and those who attend infrequently. That the more exactly controlled studies of Stoddard, Thurstone, and others showed specific and significant differences produced, complicates the question of total influence. The situation is further complicated by the fact that the producers and exhibitors have not separated the child problem from the adult problem. That is to say, they show pictures indiscriminately, to an audience consisting of minors and adults in the proportion of one minor to two adults. This causes a serious difficulty in this respect. Pictures may theoretically be satisfactory for adults and harmful to children. Presumably a much wider range of subjects and even more liberal standard for morality may be presented to adults than to children. Theoretically an adult is a free agent, but children need protection.

If, then, all pictures are constructed with only the welfare of children in mind, complications arise because adults may not be satisfied with them for themselves. Whether they should be satisfied with pictures good for children is of course a question which arouses heated controversy.

But whatever the answer, it still remains that the producers and exhibitors provide pictures for the public in general and with few exceptions they offer them as though the audiences consisted entirely of adults.

Exclusion of children from all theaters is clearly not the solution. It cannot be done because the children would crash the gate to see the thrilling scenes. Nothing of equal interest to children has happened in the world of drama before. In books, the adult drama cannot be understood by the children. In the theaters they cannot comprehend the legitimate drama. But the movie is within their comprehension and they clamor to attend.

It is inevitable, therefore, that producers of motion pictures who have a love for children and an interest in their development must address themselves to the problems of children's movies as the publishers of books have attacked the problems of providing a children's literature. Here again many problems emerge, but ingenuity will be equal to them because the welfare of children is so important. In the field of literature, scores of publishing houses produce children's books exclusively. In the field of motion pictures there undoubtedly is a place for similar institutions which would produce simply constructed pictures for children and show them in simply equipped theaters, or on special days at theaters for adults. All educators know that children's tastes are very simple; ornate pictures produced with high-salaried stars are not necessary. Theaters for children need only to be safe, sanitary, and comfortable. The experience of publishers indicates the probable success of such ventures. But whatever the solution it is evident that the producer has a direct responsibility in solving this problem.

The responsibility of course does not rest solely with the

producers, although it rests primarily with them: children now have to take what is offered to them. But parents in the presence of what we find in the theaters must exercise great care to see that their children are encouraged to see good pictures and are defended from bad ones.

The solutions of the movie problem have not been studied in these fact-finding investigations. There is no single solution nor formula that will meet the situation. The best procedure is to find the facts and publish them to stimulate discussion from which programs of action will eventually crystallize.

Certainly the problem of the movies and the children is so important and critical that parents, producers, and public must willingly and intelligently coöperate to reach some happy solution. The producers occupy the key position. The public at present must take, within the limits of the censorship of the states, whatever pictures are made.

The situation points unmistakably to the establishment by the producers of a children's department whose primary function will be to experiment, to invent, to try out, to eliminate, to press persistently until they produce proper solutions to the problem. This research organization is clearly indicated. It does not appear that such experimentation would be expensive. The simple obligation rests upon those producers who love children to find a way of making the motion picture a beautiful, fascinating, and kindly servant of childhood.

INDEX

Adult discount, 42f.
Appreciation and criticism of movies by children, 59
Attendance at movies, 5, 44ff.
Attitudes, of movie fans, 14ff.; cumulative effect upon, 21ff.; effect of one exposure upon, 20; influence of movies upon, 5, 11; measures of, 18ff.; permanence of effect upon, 23ff.
Authority of movies in child life, 9, 40f.

Blumer, Herbert, 2, 3, 4, 10, 13, 16, 23, 24, 29, 31, 36, 37, 40, 41, 42, 43, 47, 51, 61

Conclusions, 60ff.
Conduct, influence of movies upon 5, 35ff.; of movie fans, 12ff.
Conflict of movies with mores, 55ff.; aggressiveness of girls in love-making, 53f., 57f.; democratic attitudes, 57; kissing and caressing, 57; treatment of children, 57
Content of current movies, 5, 47ff.; effects of upon delinquents, 54f.; goals of characters in, 52f.; liquor in, 52f.; love, sex, and crime in, 49ff.; sex details in, 51f.; types of criminal in, 49f.; weapons in, 50f.
Cressey, Paul G., 2, 3, 12, 13, 36

Dale, Edgar, 3, 43, 44, 47, 48, 50, 52, 59, 61
Dysinger, W. S., 3, 9, 25, 27, 28, 31

Emotional detachment, 42f.
Emotional possession, 38ff.
Emotions, influence of movies upon, 5, 25, 29; danger, conflict or tragedy, 26; erotic scenes, 26ff.

Good pictures, definition of, 58

Hauser, Philip M., 2, 3, 36
Health, influence of movies upon, 5, 31
Holaday, P. W., 7, 10, 11, 27, 31, 40

Individual differences, 27, 34f.
Information, amount remembered, 8; how long remembered, 8; influence of movies upon, 5, 7ff.; what is best remembered, 10ff.
Initiation of the studies, 1

Limitations of movie influence, 17ff., 61

Marquis, Dorothy P., 3, 31
May, Mark A., 2, 4, 11, 14, 16, 17, 61
Miller, Vernon L., 3, 31
Motion Picture Research Council, 1, 2, 3, 4, 7, 56
Movies referred to: *Alibi*, 20, 21; *All Quiet on the Western Front*, 20, 21, 22, 23; *Big House*, 20, 21, 22; *Charlie Chan's Chance*, 26; *Fighting Caravans*, 7; *Four Sons*, 20, 21; *Hide Out*, 20, 21; *His Woman*, 26; *Hop to it, Bell Hop*, 25; *Journey's End*, 20, 21, 22; *New Moon*, 7; *Numbered Men*, 20, 21, 22; *Passion Flower*, 7; *Rango*, 7; *Son of the Gods*, 20, 23, 24; *Stolen Heaven*, 7; *Street of Chance*, 20, 21; *The Birth of a Nation*, 20, 21; *The Criminal Code*, 20, 21, 22; *The Feast of Ishtar*, 26, 27; *The Iron Mule*, 26; *The Road to Singapore*, 26; *The Valiant*, 20, 21; *The Yellow Ticket*, 26; *Tom Sawyer*, 7, 9; *Welcome Danger*, 20, 21

Peters, Charles C., 47, 51, 52, 55, 56, 57, 58, 59, 61
Peterson, Ruth C., 2, 11, 17, 18, 23, 31, 40
Plan of the studies, 4ff.

65

GETTING IDEAS
FROM THE MOVIES

❖

PERRY W. HOLADAY

INDIANAPOLIS PUBLIC SCHOOLS

and

GEORGE D. STODDARD

DIRECTOR, IOWA CHILD WELFARE RESEARCH STATION,
THE STATE UNIVERSITY OF IOWA

NEW YORK
THE MACMILLAN COMPANY
1933

ACKNOWLEDGMENTS

Dr. W. W. Charters of Ohio State University, director of the series of motion picture experiments of which this is one, has greatly facilitated the organization and accomplishment of the later portion of the study. Mrs. Elva Porter and others were of considerable assistance in the construction, administration, and evaluation of tests. The Ohio Censorship Board and the Columbus, Ohio, representatives of two motion picture corporations are to be thanked for the previews of pictures. Lastly, the authors wish to express their appreciation to the several thousand observers who entered so whole-heartedly into the experiment.

TABLE OF CONTENTS

LIST OF TABLES

GETTING IDEAS FROM THE MOVIES

CHAPTER I

ORGANIZATION OF THE INVESTIGATION

A description of the aims of the study.—This investigation is an attempt to measure two effects of motion pictures on the memories of children: the retention of film content and the changes in quantity and accuracy of general information, including the direction and duration of the changes. What scenes in a picture stay best in a child's memory? To what degree are geography, history, and other information subjects incidentally taught by pictures created primarily for entertainment? These effects were studied by testing children on the content of selected motion pictures to which they had been sent.

The original impetus.—This study was one of a group of studies made for the purpose of investigating the effect of motion pictures on children.[1] The problem was subdivided into several parts, and each was placed in the hands of a research expert who was allotted sufficient funds to develop his particular division according to an outline which he had previously prepared. The method of investigation for this portion of the problem was originally outlined by George D. Stoddard, and the preliminary steps of the experiment were organized around his outline. As originally planned, the study consisted of an investigation into the amounts and

[1] This series is entitled "Motion Pictures and Youth." The studies reported are listed on page ii of this volume.

kinds of general information gained and the retention of specific incidents in the pictures, together with the duration of the retention of both types of information. Later, it was found possible to carry on related investigations with profit to the study and without interfering with the essential data. Since the field of investigation covered by this report was large, emphasis was placed on an analysis of tendencies rather than on a final settlement of any single portion of the problem.

More than 3,000 observers took one or more tests. There were 17 pictures and 26 tests consisting of from 30 to 64 items each, aggregating more than 20,000 testings with approximately 813,000 items attempted.

Preliminary steps in the investigation.—The first steps consisted in the development of techniques for picture analysis and test construction. Preliminary analyses were made of 17 pictures. These were written in story form, but the principal factor in each analysis was the determination of the testing possibilities of the picture. Analyses of pictures were made on two other occasions during the study. These picture analyses served three purposes: they showed whether or not the pictures were adapted to the conditions and purposes of the study; they were useful for practice in preparing questions about the different types of action shown; and they aided in the general classification of pictures according to types (emotional, humorous, and the like) and according to use in testing.

As a further preliminary step in the experiment, two pictures, "The Gaucho" and "The Baby Cyclone," were selected for experimental analysis and test construction. Each picture was analyzed by a number of persons who were expert in dramatics, in art and architecture, or in domestic science, as well as by a stenographer and by one of the investigators. Each observed items which fell within his field. The dramatic critic wrote characterizations of the principal actors, in which he mentioned as many illustrations from the picture as possible. The art teacher and the domestic-science expert gave descriptions of clothing, furnishings, and modes of transportation. The stenographer wrote a brief summary of the plot and copied the titles and subheadings. The investigator listed items of historical, geographical, scientific, or general interest which might have been missed by the others.

From the material produced by these analyses, tests of the type used in the first three pictures were carried far enough to insure the value of the technique employed. These tests were not completed because they were not to be used; they were for practice only. They showed, however, that it was possible to construct tests which would measure adequately the main factual items of a picture. This plan for the construction of tests was continued with minor variations throughout the experiment. In September, 1929, another picture, "The Dance of Life," was similarly analyzed, and a few trial questions formulated.

Tests for the first picture.—The observation of the first picture used in the experiment, "Sorrell and Son," was carried out as just described. A complete analysis of the picture was prepared as a basis for the construction of two tests, one of general and one of specific information. The general-information test consisted of 25 yes-no items and 10 multiple-choice items, covering the customs, history, and life in England during the period shown in the picture. All questions could be answered after seeing the picture if they were not known previously, but any of them could have been answered by a well-informed individual who had not seen the picture. Examples of these questions are:

Yes-no test—

————Are there large hotels anywhere except in America? ("Sorrell and Son," General, Part 1, No. 15.) The directions for this test ask the subject to write "yes" or "no" in front of each question according to the truth or falsity of the item.

Multiple-choice test—

A famous English University is 1. Yale, 2. Harvard, 3. Princeton, 4. Oxford. ("Sorrell and Son," General, Part 2, No. 3.) The directions ask the subject to underline the correct response.[2]

The percentages of correct responses [3] on each item for each age-group on each testing showed definitely that certain changes in mental content had taken place as a result of seeing the picture. The various testings for the general-information test [4] of "Sorrell and Son" were:

Pretest—the general-information test administered before seeing the picture.

General—the same test administered to the same groups the day after the picture.

One-Month General (1 General)—the same test administered a month after the picture.

If item No. 15, Part 1, of the general-information test for "Sorrell and Son" is considered in terms of percentages of correct responses by each age-group on each testing, the following data are obtained:

[2] A very much better technique was used in later testing, as illustrated in the following question:

"A man who tried to conquer Russia and failed was   (1) Charlemagne   (2) Napoleon   (3) Achilles   (4) Wellington   (5) Mussolini.

1( )   2( )   3( )   4( )   5( )

("New Moon," General, No. 17.) The directions ask that a cross be placed in the parentheses with the same number as the correct answer. Scoring was done with a stencil laid over the test so that the correct and incorrect answers could be quickly detected and tabulated.

[3] Every effort was made to obtain the correct answer to each question; that is, the answer generally accepted by the leading authorities. In analyses of answers, the percentages of correct (accepted) answers of the entire age-group on each item were the criteria used in the evaluation of data rather than total scores of individuals within the group.

[4] Throughout the tables in this study, these designations are usually represented by the terms Pretest, General, and 1 General, respectively.

Age-Group	Percentages of Correct Responses		
	Pretest	General	1 General
Second-third grade................	10	50	84
Fifth-sixth grade.................	48	70	76
Ninth-tenth grade................	86	100	100
Adults...........................	92	96	100

There are minor eccentricities in the data, but it is noticeable that each group gained in the average amount of general information concerning this item. The Pretest was given the morning of the day the picture was seen, and the General test was given the following morning. In this interval of one day the movie was the only known variation from everyday experience. Since a similar change was found in practically every correctly shown item used in the tests, the pictures can probably be held accountable for the changes in general information. Although the item described is of minor importance, the sum total of similar items covers an important sector of human knowledge. The percentages in such tables indicate the amount of general information gained from pictures as a whole since the pictures used in the experiment constituted an adequate cross section of motion pictures.

There is frequently a maturation effect shown in these tests. As in the case of the item quoted, the memory of the picture and the utilization of the general information gained from it are occasionally better over a longer period of time than over a shorter. In this case the percentages of correct responses were higher a month after the picture than they were the day after.

The age-groups [5] used as observers in this experiment consisted of the following:

[5] The terms "second-third," "fifth-sixth," "ninth-tenth," and "adults" will be used to designate the particular section of each age-group given the test. In the various tables, the designations here given are further abbreviated to 2–3, 5–6, and 9–10.

Second-third—all available children in the second and third grades of the schools tested.

Fifth-sixth—all available children in the fifth and sixth grades of these schools.

Ninth-tenth—all available children in the ninth and tenth grades of these schools.

Adults—groups of 75 and 125 superior adults.

For each subsequent picture, with one exception, a test of specific information covering the action, background, and characterization of the movie was constructed. The specific-information tests for "Sorrell and Son" were given twice:

Specific—the specific-information test given the day following the picture.

One-Month Specific (1 Specific)—the same test administered to the same groups a month after the picture.

All tests mentioned in this report, both general- and specific-information tests, are referred to by the designations mentioned. [6] In each case, the name of the picture for which the test was constructed is appended unless it is clearly understood. The "Mysterious Island" Specific or the "Moran of the Marines" One-Month General will be understood as the specific-information test for "Mysterious Island" taken the day after the picture and of the general-information test for "Moran of the Marines" taken one month after the picture was seen. Any time element mentioned in the description of the test refers to the length of time intervening between the picture and the administration of the test. During the last year of the experiment the One-Month General (1 General) and the One-Month Specific (1 Specific) tests were replaced by the One-and-a-Half-Month General (1½ General) and Specific (1½ Specific), and a Three-Month Specific (3 Specific) was added. For one picture a Seven-Month Specific (7 Specific) was used.

[6] *See* footnote 4, page 4.

Tests for the first three pictures consisted of yes-no and four-response multiple-choice items. For the pictures of the following year the yes-no items were replaced by completion items, and the four-response multiple-choice items were replaced by those of the five-response type. An example of the completion tests used follows:

Three days later he received word that his terms were accepted, and he started to go to ————. ("General Crack," Specific, Part 1, No. 14)

Directions ask that the word necessary to complete the meaning be written in the blank. This type of testing was used for specific-information tests only. Evaluation of the efficiency of these techniques and of various additions made to the testing program will be found in the next chapter.

The 17 pictures used in the experiment were:

1928–30:
   "Sorrell and Son"—Drama of war-time and postwar England. Silent.
   "Moran of the Marines"—Humorous treatment of life in the marine corps at home and abroad. Silent.
   "The Midnight Taxi"—Light drama of crook life. Talking sequences.
   "Kitty"—Romantic drama of postwar England. Talking sequences.
   "Why Bring That Up?"—Humorous account of the rise to fame of the Two Black Crows of phonograph fame. All talking.
   "The Four Feathers"—War in the Sudan and life in England. Very good shots of native and animal life. Silent.
   "Mysterious Island"—Melodramatic phantasy of life in an undersea kingdom. Technicolor. Talking sequences.
   "Return of Sherlock Holmes"—The mysterious adventures of the famous detective. All talking.
   "Show of Shows"—A revue carried out in motion pictures. A number of scenes exploiting motion-picture stars. Mostly technicolor. All talking.

"General Crack"—Romantic drama of war and love in Austria of 1740. All talking.

1930–31: [7]

"Tom Sawyer"—The adventures of Mark Twain's boy hero and his friends.

"Passion Flower"—A drama of modern society, based upon the familiar triangle plot.

"Gang Buster"—A comedy of crooks and their actions.

"New Moon"—Musical romance of love and fighting at a frontier fort in pre-war Russia.

"Fighting Caravans"—Stirring melodrama of life in a wagon train crossing the plains in the early 1860's.

"Stolen Heaven"—Drama of Palm Beach society life.

"Rango"—Native and animal life in Sumatra. This picture is quite scenic but contains a record rather than a story. No test of specific information was used.

Summary.—This study was planned to determine the amounts of general information retained by children after viewing a motion picture and the specific incidents of the picture remembered by them over brief and long periods of time. The subjects consisted of approximately 3,000 children in the second, third, fifth, sixth, ninth, and tenth grades and 200 superior adults. All were sent to 17 motion pictures upon which they were tested. Each general-information test covered general items of information shown in the picture and was administered as a pretest the day before the picture and again the day following the picture and a month later. Each specific-information test covered the action, background, and characterization of a particular picture and was administered the day following the picture and again a month later. Certain variations in the time of testing were introduced in the last year of study.

[7] Pictures used during these years were all talking.

CHAPTER II

TECHNIQUES USED IN THE STUDY

Combinations of test data.—This experiment was based partially upon the assumption that a carefully selected group of motion pictures, embracing all current types, would constitute a fair sampling of motion pictures as a whole. This assumption was later proved empirically. If the study is so constructed that it has for a basis a cross section of the totality of motion pictures for the years 1928–30, a closer scrutiny of this cross section is in order.

A motion picture is not an entire unit by itself. A humorous picture is not entirely humorous to the exclusion of other types of material; it is simply a picture in which the element of humor predominates although other elements are present in varying and unpredictable amounts. A direct comparison upon any basis of two humorous pictures is not feasible because of this factor, for the other elements are not necessarily similar for the two pictures and may cause an unpredictable effect upon any comparisons of the total pictures. In a sense, the humorous elements of two pictures are themselves not comparable, but a comparison of these partials is a more logical step than comparisons of total pictures. If, however, the group of pictures selected for the study is described as a cross section of pictures as a whole, the situation changes. The pictures are considered as a group and assume a more unitary aspect. There is no longer any motive for comparing humorous items from picture to picture, since the entire group of humorous items from all of the pictures also assumes a unitary aspect. Comparisons are now to be found between the sum total of humorous items and the sum total of items of other types. This comparison is based upon items drawn from all pictures in the study, rather than from one alone.

For this reason the total scores of individuals on motion-picture tests are considered less important than average scores of the various age-groups on particular test items. Individual scores are based upon entire but single pictures, whereas individual items can be grouped according to definite types. This permits really important comparisons to be made throughout the entire group of pictures.

Equation of groups of observers.—During the first year and a half the study was conducted at the University of Iowa. The three youngest groups of observers were taken largely from the elementary school and the high school conducted by the University. The adults consisted largely of graduate students in the University and their wives. Some students from the Training School of Iowa State Teachers College observed several pictures and answered the tests. Pretests of "Moran of the Marines" and "The Midnight Taxi" were also given at Washington, Iowa, and Cedar Rapids, Iowa.

During the last year the experiment was conducted at Ohio State University, Columbus, Ohio. This move was taken for three reasons: First, since Columbus is the capital of Ohio, the Ohio State Division of Film Censorship is located there, and previews of pictures could be obtained at the office of the State Division or at the local district offices of two motion-picture concerns considerably in advance of the actual exhibition of the pictures. Second, it was possible at Columbus to obtain larger groups of observers who came from more varied types of communities than could be found in Iowa. Third, while obtaining the two first-named advantages, there was no loss in the administration of the study since the facilities of the Bureau of Educational Research of Ohio State University were made available for the use of the investigation.

The groups used in this portion of the experiment consisted of:

Pupils from Raschig Elementary School and Woodward High School, Cincinnati, Ohio—probably the poorest district in a large city. No Negroes were included either here or in any other of the groups.

Pupils from Avondale Elementary School and Walnut Hills High School, Cincinnati, Ohio—a high-class residential district. The high school is distinctly a college-preparatory school and draws superior students from all over the city.

Pupils from Heyl Avenue Elementary School and South High School, Columbus, Ohio—a middle-class district in a large city.

Pupils from the elementary schools and high school, Delaware, Ohio—a small town built around Ohio Wesleyan University.

Pupils from the elementary schools and high school, Wellsburg, West Virginia—a small town in the coal and iron district. There is also a small amount of manufacturing.

Pupils from the elementary schools and high school, Jackson, Mississippi—a town of fifty thousand located in a district which is largely agricultural..

Superior adults, Columbus, Ohio—principally graduate students or young professors. .

Thus a sampling of students from six types of communities with a wide range in home life and in occupational and financial status was obtained. The pictures were the same for all localities, and the mimeographed tests were administered under the same conditions. Variations in the test results should, to a large extent, represent variations in communities, and a combination of the data from all localities, comprising the tests taken by a total of over two thousand elementary- and high-school students, should provide an adequate sampling and should represent approximately the findings which would be obtained by a similar study in any group of American communities.

For the first picture of the experiment, "Sorrell and Son," all observers for the picture were given all the tests, but this proved to be a poor arrangement. It is difficult to administer a test to a child satisfactorily more than once. In particular, the Pretest should not be administered to students who are later to answer the General or the 1 General. After taking the examination an observer goes to the motion picture with a changed attitude. He is conditioned. As certain sections of the play unfold themselves, he recognizes questions he was asked previously and remembers the answers. These high points stay in his memory to a far larger degree than would be the case if he had attended the play with the sole motive and interest of personal enjoyment. For similar reasons, a test cannot be repeated for an observer after the picture, even though the two tests are a month apart, since the asking of a question based upon a portion of a picture raises that scene to a higher level of recall than the scenes which are unmentioned. At the end of a month it is doubtful whether the scene will have faded much, if at all, as the results of "Sorrell and Son" showed, and questions regarding it may even be answered with a higher degree of accuracy than immediately following the picture.

For these reasons, all the observers in each age-group were equated into three sections, A, B, and C, on the basis of age, intelligence, and reading ability. The three sections of each test were then administered to the A, B, and C groups at each age-level separately. For instance, the Pretest and Specific for one picture were given to Group A, the General and 1½ Specific to Group B, and the 1½ General and 3 Specific to C. The groups at each age-level were considered approximately equivalent, and the differences in the average scores of the A group (taking the Pretest) and the B group (taking the General the day after the picture) were attributed to the effect of the picture. Similar differences between the General and the 1½ General and among the sections of the specific-information tests were considered indications of the quantity and quality of the retention of the general and specific information furnished by the picture. In the light of other innovations to be described in the remainder of this section and, also, in that of empirical data, likewise described, these assumptions are justified.

All equating was done on the person-to-person basis; observers were paired according to age and all test scores obtainable for the age-group. These sections within an age-group were retained for all pictures seen by that group. In theory, practically equivalent motion-picture test results should have been expected from three sections within an age-group if they had been shown the picture at the same time and tested under the same conditions. To increase the probability of equality between the three sections of each age-group, they were rotated. If Section A took the Pretest for one picture, it was given the General for the next picture and the 1 General for the one following; Sections B and C were varied similarly. Rotation of groups was also done with tests of specific information. On the several occasions when it was possible to test two or all three of these equated sections in each age-group on the same test, practically equal average scores were obtained (see Table II).

The average ages, mental ages, reading ages, and intelligence quotients of all the sections are given in Table I. This table shows that there were no large discrepancies between two of the three sections of any age-group in any locality.

TABLE I

AVERAGE AGES, READING AGES, MENTAL AGES, AND INTELLIGENCE QUOTIENTS FOR ALL GROUPS

	GRADES 2–3	GRADES 5–6	GRADES 9–10	ADULTS
Data from the 1929–30 Study a				
	Chronological Ages			
Cedar Falls:				
A....................	8–3	10–11	15–0	......
Iowa City:				
B....................	8–4	10– 9	14–3	31–0
C....................	8–2	10– 8	14–3	26–8
D....................	8–1	......	......	27–7
	Mental Ages			
Cedar Falls:				
A....................	9–6	11–11	16– 6	......
Iowa City:				
B....................	10–0	12– 9	14– 9	......
C....................	9–8	12–11	14–11	......
D....................	9–2	......	......	......
	Intelligence Quotients			
Cedar Falls:				
A....................	115	109	110	......
Iowa City:				
B....................	119 ·	120	107	......
C....................	117	122 ·	111	......
D....................	113	......	......	......
	Reading Ages or Scores			
Cedar Falls:				
A....................	9– 4	......	...... b	......
Iowa City:				
B....................	10– 6	......	14.32	29.16 c
C....................	9–11	......	13.29	28.92
D....................	9–10	......	......	28.42

a All existing data are included. Blanks indicate that information is not available for that group.

b Scores on the Carpenter English Test.

c Scores on the Iowa Comprehension Test.

TABLE I (*Continued*)

AVERAGE AGES, READING AGES, MENTAL AGES, AND
INTELLIGENCE QUOTIENTS FOR ALL GROUPS (*Continued*)

	GRADES 2–3	GRADES 5–6	GRADES 9–10	ADULTS
Data from the 1930–31 Study [a]				
	Chronological Ages			
Jackson:				
A......................	6–11	10– 4	14– 7	......
B......................	6– 8	10– 2	14– 7	......
C......................	7– 1	10– 6	14– 7	......
Columbus:				
A......................	8– 2	10–11	15– 2	28–9
B......................	8– 9	11– 0	15– 1	29–5
C......................	8– 2	11– 4	14– 7	28–6
Delaware:				
A......................	7– 8	10– 6	14–10	......
B......................	6– 8	9– 9	14–10	......
C......................	6– 6	10– 9	15– 2	......
Wellsburg:				
A......................	8– 4	11– 8	15– 4	......
B......................	8– 8	11– 6	15– 2	......
C......................	8– 8	11– 3	15– 3	......
Avondale and Walnut Hills:				
A......................	7–10	10–10	14– 1	......
B......................	7–10	10– 9	14– 1	......
C......................	7–11	10–10	14– 0	......
Raschig and Woodward:				
A......................	7–10	12– 8	......	......
B......................	8–10	12– 2	......	......
C......................	8–10	12– 4	......	......
	Mental Ages			
Columbus:				
A......................	8– 1	......	14–11	......
B......................	7– 7	......	14–11	......
C......................	7– 9	......	14–10	......
Avondale:				
A......................	......	11–4	......	......
B......................	......	11–1	......	......
C......................	......	11–3	......	......
	Scores on Stanford Reading			
Jackson:				
A......................	59	158	207	......
B......................	58	161	194	......
C......................	59	159	206	......

[a] All existing data are included. Blanks indicate that information is not available
for that group.

15

TABLE I (*Continued*)

AVERAGE AGES, READING AGES, MENTAL AGES, AND INTELLIGENCE QUOTIENTS FOR ALL GROUPS (*Continued*)

	GRADES 2–3	GRADES 5–6	GRADES 9–10	ADULTS
	Scores on Stanford Achievement Test			
Raschig:				
A....................	32	71	......	....
B....................	32	71	......	....
C....................	33	70	......	....
	Intelligence Quotients			
Columbus:				
A....................	101	......	99	....
B....................	95	......	100	....
C....................	97	......	102	....
Avondale:				
A....................	......	104	......	....
B....................	......	107	......	....
C....................	......	105	......	....
Woodward:				
A....................	......	......	102	....
B....................	......	......	101	....
C....................	......	......	101	....
	Scores on Otis Group Intelligence Scale [d]			
Jackson:				
A....................	45.9	......	......	......
B....................	46.2	......	......	......
C....................	47.3	......	......	....
	Scores on Otis Self-Administering Test [e]			
Jackson:				
A....................	......	43.0	45.9	59.3
B....................	......	44.8	46.3	56.5
C....................	......	43.3	45.8	60.3
	Scores on Terman Group Test			
Wellsburg:				
A....................	......	......	121.7	....
B....................	......	......	120.8	....
C....................	......	......	115.8	....

[d] Primary.
[e] Intermediate and higher.

In three cases the pictures were exhibited in the local theaters so near the close of school that it was impossible to give the tests a month and a half or three months after the picture. Some of the groups which would normally be given these tests were therefore given the Specific tests for the two pictures. The average score for each group is given in Table II. The probable errors of the difference show but little difference between groups. Of the 15 possible comparisons of groups at the same age-level, 9 show differences of less than 1 PE, which might be expected by chance, and none approaches 4 PE, which would indicate certainty of differences.

From these experiments it may well be assumed that the three sections of age-group were practically equivalent; and, in consequence, the rotation of sections, the administration of the different testings of each age-group, and the combination of test results obtained from different sections are all valid proceedings.

Types of testing techniques employed.—Several techniques were utilized in the process of discovering those best adapted to this type of research. For the first picture three techniques were used. The mimeographed tests given to older children and adults were of the yes-no (true-false) type in Part 1 and four-response multiple-choice type in Part 2. Part 1 only was read to the children of the second-third grade-group, and they wrote the answers "yes" or "no" on sheets of paper which they had previously numbered. In addition, every child and adult was asked to write a ten-minute essay on the plot of the story, which was written before the taking of the tests given after the picture. The themes were dropped for the next two pictures although the same form of objective testing was retained.

The essays were exceptionally difficult to administer and

to evaluate. The total number of facts mentioned by the second grade [1] averaged only 4.9 per student, while for the adults the average per observer was 42.9 facts. This is comprehensible when it is considered that, in addition to differences between these groups in the ability to understand the

TABLE II

THE STATISTICAL SIGNIFICANCE OF THE DIFFERENCES BETWEEN AVERAGE SCORES OF THE A, B, AND C GROUPS ON THE SPECIFIC TESTS FOR TWO PICTURES

	GROUP A	GROUP B	GROUP C	PROBABLE ERROR OF DIFFERENCE		
				Groups A and B	Groups A and C	Groups B and C
"New Moon"						
Grades 2–3:						
Raschig.........	....	20.83	20.21	....	....	.68
Avondale.......	....	23.98	21.39	....	....	3.14
Grades 5–6:						
Raschig.........	....	26.95	25.82	....	....	.97
Avondale.......	....	25.77	26.79	....	....	1.25
Grades 9–10:						
Woodward......	....	31.26	31.74	....	....	.57
Walnut Hills....	....	30.71	29.64	....	....	.72
"Stolen Heaven"						
Wellsburg:						
Grades 2–3.....	22.42	22.96	23.70	.47	1.31	.97
Grades 5–6.....	23.00	24.22	23.72	1.20	.70	.58
Grades 9–10....	28.79	30.97	31.17	1.81	2.10	.24

pictures, there was added the further differences in ability to express thoughts in complex forms of written language, to organize a story, and to concentrate on an abstract operation of this sort for a ten-minute period. There is a certain

[1] Data for the second grade are tabulated separately from those of the third in this one instance in the study.

relationship between ability to answer a test on a movie and to write a theme about it. Correlations between the number of facts given in themes and the scores on General or Specific tests for "Sorrell and Son" were low but positive. The themes varied from the following contribution in the second grade, "it was interesting, i thought," to the polished, typed synopses written by graduate students. The total number of facts from each age-group were classified according to seventeen categories—the thirteen scenes of the picture, the names of characters, comments on the picture, mistakes, and items which could not be classified in one of the other groups. Responses varied considerably, for observers in each age-group commented on what to them seemed to be the most pertinent items. Mistakes in fact were far more common for younger children than for adults. Statistical treatment was impossible with these data.

One further attempt at the theme technique was made during the testing of the picture "Kitty." Adult observers were asked to describe the relations existing between Kitty and her mother-in-law. Possibly, because of the limited range of the topic or the subjective type of topic, the themes were even more difficult to analyze than were those for "Sorrell and Son," and the attempt to adapt this type of questioning to the uses of the study was abandoned.

The true-false type of item is not thoroughly usable for research of this type. In theory, correction for guessing makes the true-false item a valid type to use; and where the main point of interest is the obtaining of the relative standings of various individuals in an academic course, the true-false question is satisfactory. In this study, the main emphasis is not upon individual scores, which are practically disregarded, but upon percentages of correct responses upon each item. When a test of general information is given as a pretest preceding the picture for which it was constructed, the true-false type of question might yield satisfactory results; when the same test is administered to groups which have seen the picture, however, many of the effects of the picture upon the observers are lost in the corrections for chance usually in use with true-false questions. Consider for an instant a hypothetical test item. If the tests for "The Mysterious Island," a movie containing many contrary-to-fact situations, had been constructed partly or entirely of the yes-no type, one question might have been worded: "Can a submarine receive radio messages while it is 100 feet deep under the water?" According to physics this is an impossibility,[2] yet the action is shown in the picture. In an adult group which had seen the picture, there might be 40 per cent who were certain of the facts of the case and still responded "no" regardless of the action shown on the screen, while an additional 20 per cent were uncertain and half answered "yes" and half "no," and the remaining 40 per cent accepted the movie as an authority and answered "yes." The answers of the ones who really knew the accepted answer would be lost as the percentage of correct responses would be 50 per cent minus 50 per cent or zero, whereas there were 40 per cent of the group really conversant with the true facts of the case. This is an exaggerated, but perfectly possible, situation. Another item might receive a much larger percentage of correct answers than it deserves because of its wording. If a question had been asked in this same test: "Was the first successful submarine built by the English?" the correct answer would be "no," as the honor is usually ascribed to Robert Fulton, an American, who constructed a ship of this type for the French government.

[2] Morecroft, J. D., *Principles of Radio Communication*, 2d ed., London, John Wiley and Sons, 1927, p. 843.

Although only 40 per cent of those who saw the picture really knew the history of the first submarine, an additional 50 per cent might easily consider the pictorial construction of such a ship by a race allied to the Russians as a historical fact and likewise answer "no," giving the percentage right as 40 per cent plus 50 per cent, or 90 per cent, and the corrected percentage 90 per cent minus 10 per cent or 80 per cent instead of 40 per cent. Because of these possible variations, the true-false type of item was eliminated.

The four-response multiple-choice type permits a small amount of guessing, and it was therefore changed to the five-response form to minimize the guessing element still further. Items of the completion or recall type were introduced to replace the yes-no questions, but they were dropped in the 1930–31 portion of the study because the form of the question made it more difficult to answer than a multiple-choice question of equal difficulty of content. Data based upon the two types could not validly be combined.

In several of the following tables it will appear that the retention of second-third grade children at times surpasses that of older children and occasionally even that of adults. That is, of course, fallacious and results from the form of the tests rather than from actual conditions. At least four factors enter into this situation, three of them definitely favoring the youngest group and the fourth unpredictable. The first two listed appear in the 1929–30 portion of the study only and are doubtless the factors which cause the apparent strength of the youngest group during this period. This strength is not so noticeable in the 1930–31 portion where these factors did not operate.

First, during 1929–30 shortened forms of tests were employed for the second-third grade-group. For the first three pictures, the older observers were given yes-no and multiple-choice questions, while the youngest group received only the yes-no questions. During the next year, 30 or 32 questions were selected from the 40 or 64 questions of each complete test and were adapted to the use of the second-third rank. The complex situations of the picture were avoided, and, as a result, since the questions asked the younger group were easier than the ones not asked them the average scores of the older groups were lower comparatively. This was proved by statistical analysis. The questions asked the second-third grade-group were easier for all older observers than the questions not asked the younger group. These questions which were easier in the first place also had a higher degree of retention for older observers. This was true for both specific- and general-information tests.

Second, the questions were not placed in the same form for second-third grade and older observers. During the 1929–30 portion of the study the multiple-choice type of item was used exclusively with the second-third grade-group, while the completion type, which is harder, was used at least half of the time in the specific-information tests for older observers.

Third, the second-third grade-group received all its questions in the form of three-response multiple-choice questions, while the multiple-choice questions for older observers were five-response. Because of the difficulties of testing which these children met and the fact that they are naïve as regards tests of this type, no correction was made for guessing. This is empirical reasoning, but there is a certain amount of proof to support this step. During the testing on "New Moon" at Cincinnati, equated groups at each age-level were tested simultaneously with three-response and five-response tests of both specific and general information. The three-response test was 20 per cent easier for the second-third grade-group, but only 2 per cent easier for the adults. No corrections for guessing were made.

Finally, the second-third grade-group had their questions read to them, while all older observers were furnished mimeographed copies of the test. The comparative difficulty of these two procedures is open to question.

Methods employed in obtaining and evaluating material.— The methods of analysis and test construction used in the early pictures have been discussed previously. Commencing with "The Mysterious Island," another technique for analysis was necessary because films were unavailable for previews and had to be seen in more or less distant communities which were favored with an exhibition before Iowa City. Changes in technique of analysis were necessary for two reasons. In the first place, it was difficult to organize a group of experts for long trips. Second, analyses of tests used for previous pictures showed that there were few questions in these tests which could not have been constructed from the data furnished by the author and his assistants. The best method was found to be that summarized in the following paragraphs:

1. The picture was seen at least once, but preferably twice by the author and his assistants, who took all the notes they could, and were assisted by a stenographer who timed the scenes.

2. As many items as possible which would furnish test questions were listed from the combined notes of the three persons. All points at which speech, action, or background were remembered or interpreted differently by two observers were noted. Any large portion of the film which had no questions to cover it was noted.

3. The observers saw the picture once, two or more times if possible, and the list of test items was subsequently revised.

4. When the type of pictures exhibited made it possible, the observers read the novel from which the movie had been

adapted, as well as histories, geographies, or other books which would give a clearer view of the actual conditions existing at the time and place of the setting. Experts from different departments of the University of Iowa were consulted on technical points of history, physics, and geography.

5. The tests were constructed by the experimenters; checked by the technical experts referred to in the previous section; checked as to the distribution of the questions throughout the movie; checked by the director of the study; and then at the proper time administered to the observers in mimeographed form.

For the second and third grades it was deemed advisable to use items which were phrased in less complex language than were those used for adults. In the first three pictures this factor was cared for by the procedure of asking the children to write "yes" or "no" to the items which were read to them, and only Part 1 (yes-no items) was given in these grades. For later pictures special tests consisting of 30 or 32 three-response items were constructed, in which each item was based upon a similar one from the mimeographed completion or five-choice items. When a five-choice item was reduced to three-choice, the changes necessary to prepare it for second-third use usually consisted only of deletion of two choices.

During 1930–31 the tests were constructed with the same care. Previews were obtained at the Ohio State Division of Film Censorship or at the district offices of film companies, and tests were constructed before exhibition of the pictures. First exhibitions usually took place at Jackson, Mississippi, with the Cincinnati showings in a neighborhood theater approximately two months later. Owing to this unavoidable difference in schedule, Jackson was the only locality in which all the tests for all the pictures were administered. "Tom Sawyer" is the only picture during 1930–31 for which all returns are available from all groups.

Care was taken in all tests to make the items as objective as possible. The place of the correct answer in the multiple-choice item was determined principally by chance, yet the correct responses of the whole section of the test were placed in equal numbers in each of the possible three, four, or five locations. All incorrect responses were logical, but fine discriminations were avoided. Whenever possible, the item was so written that the confused elements were actually present or possible in the play but not in conjunction with the incident questioned. An incomplete recall of the incident would likely lead to memory of another section of the picture and consequently to a missed answer. In a similar manner, the completion items were carefully constructed so that no question was preceded by either "a" or "an," which might give a hint as to whether the desired response commenced with a vowel or a consonant. All questions were proof read many times to be certain that no alternative answers were possible. As a result of this care, only a few of the 868 questions in the tests for the last 14 pictures used appear to be open to interpretation other than that intended at the time of their construction.

Validation of tests.—Among the outstanding methods of validating material of this type are:

1. By judgment of competent persons.
2. By analysis of pictures.
3. By computation of percentages of the pupils answering each item correctly at each successive age-level.
4. By correlation against outside criteria.
5. By correlation with another form of the test.
6. By combination of these items.[3]

[3] Adapted from Ruch, G. M., and Stoddard, G. D., *Tests and Measurements in High School Instruction*, Yonkers-on-Hudson, N. Y.: World Book Co., 1927. Pp. xix, 381. (P. 29.)

The judgment of competent persons was involved in the construction of the tests, and the analysis of pictures has already been mentioned. The percentages of pupils answering each item correctly at each successive age-level will be reported in the following chapter, together with the other findings of the study.

There are no outside criteria in this case. The closest approach is in the case of "Sorrell and Son," where themes were written by the children previous to the answering of the tests. This is really correlation with another form of the test. The chief problem here lies in the analysis of the themes into units comparable to those of the tests. Themes may be correlated with test results in two ways. Total test scores may be compared to the number of facts given in the themes written in the same group. The tests used in the comparison are Part 1 and the total forms for both general and specific tests. None of the correlations is high, the highest (General, Part 1 and second-third-grade themes) being .58, while the correlation between the adult themes and the same test is 0. Probably low correlations are due to three factors: the tests for this picture have only medium reliability; the tests were not as carefully constructed as for later pictures and the time divisions (according to scenes) of the picture were not covered as uniformly as later; the method used to analyze themes is open to question as some observers gave facts in detail and with much elaboration, while others confined themselves to simple statements of the details of the plot. In a ten-minute theme, an observer of the first type might easily indicate a more thorough knowledge of the picture than an observer of the second type who gave twice the number of classifiable facts. Another factor which should be mentioned here is the fact that this early test did not have enough "top" for adult observers. Many scores approached the highest possible score, thus concealing individual differences.

In later tests, from "Why Bring That Up?" on, each movie was timed with a stop watch, and the contents of the picture correlated with the contents of the tests according to two methods. In one, the amount of time in each scene was compared to the number of test items covering the scene. All correlations were high, ranging from .66 to .92, showing that the tests covered approximately the material of the pictures. In the 1930–31 study, all tests were so constructed that correlations of this type ranged from .94 to 1.00. It should be mentioned at this point that each set of tests for a picture carried one to four or even more questions concerning the names of actors, the film company producing the picture, or the author who wrote the play. The titles for the picture were exhibited from 45 seconds to a minute only, and since each test has this comparison of a fraction of a percentage of time covered by about 6 per cent of the questions, all correlations are smaller than they could easily be made by the elimination of this type of test item.

For the second type of comparison, all test questions in the 1929–30 portion of the study were divided into ten categories, according to the type of action going on at the time. These categories were:

1. Emotion—all scenes of a highly emotional nature, except fighting, mysterious, or romantic types of action.
2. Humor—all scenes of a humorous nature.
3. Mystery—all scenes of a mysterious or supernatural nature, including scenes of the detective-story type.
4. Revue—all scenes of public entertainment, exhibition dancing or stage.
5. Crime—all scenes of planned or executed crime.
6. Fighting—all scenes of personal combat or of war.
7. Romance—all scenes of love-making, marriage, and the like.

8. Drinking—all cabaret (excepting Type 4) or other scenes where drinking was shown, used in general tests only.

9. General conversation—all scenes where there is no action of the preceding types occurring, and groups are engaged in ordinary conversation, usually leading up to one of the types of action previously mentioned. Titles, names of producers, authors, and actors are included here.

10. General action—all action of such a general nature that it can be included in none of the categories just given.

Examples of questions of these types,[4] taken from tests of specific information, with the exception of the item on drinking, are:

1. Emotion—The hussars tortured Sonia by   (1) burning her with a hot iron   (2) pulling her hair   (3) hurting her brother while she was watching   (4) hitting her   (5) <u>crushing her ankles</u> ("The Mysterious Island," Part 1, No. 3).

2. Humor—Mack said that he had   (1) two   (2) four   (3) <u>five</u> (4) ten   (5) fifteen cats, and had cut a hole in the door for each one of them ("Why Bring That Up?" Part 1, No. 32).

3. Mystery—The thing which led the undersea people to attack the men in diving suits was <u>the taste of blood</u> ("The Mysterious Island," Part 2, No. 4).

4. Revue—When Holmes did some sleight-of-hand tricks at the entertainment, he took   (1) a watch   (2) <u>a bill</u>   (3) a handkerchief (4) a hairpin   (5) a key from a lady, apparently destroyed it, and then gave it back safely ("The Return of Sherlock Holmes," Part 2, No. 10).

5. Crime—Holmes said that it was not an ordinary robbery since (1) the silverware was not taken   (2) the gun had not been fired   (3) the boy was gone   (4) <u>the safe had not been touched</u> (5) the policeman couldn't find any clues ("The Return of Sherlock Holmes," Part 2, No. 9).

6. Fighting—The natives stopped fighting and ran away because <u>their chief had been killed</u> ("The Four Feathers," Part 2, No. 8).

7. Romance—General Crack said that the most precious thing in the world to him was   (1) power   (2) the palace at Ottenheim (3) Marie Louisa   (4) the Kurland diamonds   (5) <u>Fidelia's kiss</u> ("General Crack," Part 2, No. 20).

---

[4] If several answers are given, the item is of the multiple-choice variety and the correct answer is underlined. If only one answer is given, the item is of a completion variety and the correct answer is underlined. In the former test the child was required to underline the answer which he believed correct; in the latter he wrote in an answer in the blank space provided.

8. Drinking—In those days, the people of Austria drank principally (1) water   (2) coffee   (3) wine   (4) tea   (5) whiskey ("General Crack," General No. 10).
9. General Conversation—The Duke said that the sound of cannon made him   (1) angry   (2) afraid   (3) sad   (4) homesick   (5) happy ("General Crack," Part 2, No. 2).
   —This movie was made by   (1) Metro-Goldwyn   (2) Fox   (3) Warner Bros.   (4) Universal   (5) Paramount ("Why Bring That Up?" Part 1, No. 2).
10. General Action—Frank Fay announced the next act. He was dressed in a soldier's uniform and wore a number of medals ("Show of Shows," No. 6).

In classifying items, the reference is not to the question itself, but to the action carried on in the particular portion of the picture covered by the question. For example in the item

When Moran was talking to Betty about the jewelry he had bought her, he called it   (1) ice   (2) fruit   (3) liquid fire   (4) glass   (5) cards ("Why Bring That Up?" Part 1, No. 23).

there is apparently nothing but general conversation, yet the movie at this point shows a man who is desperate because he realizes that the girl he loves has been playing with him, has influenced him to steal from his partner, has caused injury and possible death to his partner. The question is therefore classified as emotional. All items given as illustrations are quite clear-cut as to type, and there are many others that can be classified with similar ease. However, in the case of certain questions the classifications necessarily rest upon the judgments of three persons who saw the movies many times and, with the aid of others, constructed the tests. The judgments were admittedly subjective. Definite instructions for classifying the items were formulated and followed by the three observers, and all the judgments were agreed to by all observers. The sectioning of items rested probably upon the expert opinion available at the time.

Three methods were used in correlating the items from the 1929–30 tests and the content of selected films. All three experiments tried showed high relationship between the percentages of the various kinds of action found in test items and in movies in general. This classification will again be referred to in connection with the analysis of results. The classifications used in this section are not intended to be all-inclusive, but simply to cover all the action of the pictures used.

As a further check on the validity of the testing, a number of children and adults were given both the oral and the usual mimeographed test for "Stolen Heaven." Oral testing was done individually and preceded the written test. The examiner was provided with a list of the 40 questions included in the mimeographed Specific test. The subject was asked to tell the story of the picture. Each question of those in the test answered voluntarily, whether correctly or incorrectly, was so checked by the examiner. After the story had been told, the examiner went back over the test and asked the questions which had been omitted, using a standardized wording for each question. No list of possible solutions was presented; the questions were entirely of the recall type. After all children included in the experiment had been thus tested, all were given the regular mimeographed Specific test. This procedure was followed for 34 children from Avondale and Woodward High School at Cincinnati and 17 adults, 30 children from the Bureau of Juvenile Research at Columbus (Specific), and 23 children from Heyl and South High at Columbus (1½ Specific). The data from this experiment as given in Table III definitely show that the questions constructed to cover the picture are the ones answered in the telling of the story of the picture. Reliabilities are not furnished for the third group, the 1½ Spe-

cific for Columbus, as only a few children were available
at each age-level.

In the case of the students tested on the oral test for
"Stolen Heaven," the children from the best district at
Cincinnati had average scores on both oral and written
tests lower than those of the corresponding groups from the
Bureau of Juvenile Research. The children in this institution
are committed there as being either disciplinary or social-
problem cases, and they live under the constant restriction of
an institution. They saw the picture under less favorable
conditions, and they were less familiar with the methods used
in testing. In addition to having higher scores than the
public-school children, they had reliabilities nearly as high,
and for two out of three age-groups, there was a higher percentage on the oral tests as compared to the written.

This experiment showed several things: First, there was a
high relationship between actual retention of the picture and
scores on formal written tests. Second, the scores on oral
tests were approximately 85 per cent as high as scores on
written tests. Third, the findings of this study apply to all
types of subjects. When the proper stimuli (the mimeographed tests used in this study) are applied, the details
and action of a picture can be recalled with a high degree
of accuracy, regardless of the make-up of the group of subjects. Finally, these tests cover quite accurately the material
of the picture. The validity of the tests is satisfactory if
the following facts are kept in mind: (1) the tests possessed
sufficient range to accommodate both second-grade children and university graduates; (2) there was no opportunity
for revision or standardization as tests were used as soon
as constructed; (3) the tests were short, being only 40 to
60 questions long, on account of the length of school time
available for their administration.

TABLE III

A COMPARISON OF AVERAGE PERCENTAGES OF CORRECT
RESPONSES ON ORAL AND WRITTEN SPECIFIC TESTS
FOR "STOLEN HEAVEN"

Group	Type of Test	Grades 2–3	Grades 5–6	Grades 9–10	Adults
Oral test:					
Cincinnati............	Specific	44.4	69.3	78.4	74.6
Bureau of Juvenile Research..............	Specific	52.9	73.9	83.1	....
Columbus............	1½ Specific	40.0	53.8	63.1	....
Written test:					
Cincinnati............	Specific	62.1	76.6	84.8	80.9
Bureau of Juvenile Research..............	Specific	63.7	79.9	86.3	....
Columbus............	1½ Specific	49.3	66.3	68.8	....
Percentage oral is of written:					
Cincinnati............	Specific	71.5	90.5	92.5	92.2
Bureau of Juvenile Research..............	Specific	83.0	72.5	96.3	....
Columbus............	1½ Specific	81.1	81.1	91.7	....
Measures of Reliability of Test					
Oral test:					
Cincinnati............	Specific	.69	.56	.29	.90
Bureau of Juvenile Research..............	Specific	.53	.74	.83	....
Written test:					
Cincinnati............	Specific	.85	.85	.82	.70
Bureau of Juvenile Research..............	Specific	.64	.80	.86	....
Correlation of oral with written:					
Cincinnati	Specific	.92	.73	.66	.84
Bureau of Juvenile Research..............	Specific	.82	.78	.88	....

This table should be read as follows: Children in the second-third grade-group at Cincinnati answered 44.4 per cent of the questions on the oral test and 62.1 per cent of the questions on the written test, or they were 71.5 per cent as high on the oral as on the written test, and so on. The reliabilities of the oral tests are not so high as those of the written tests, but the correlations between scores on oral and written tests are quite high.

Reliability of tests.—The reliabilities of these tests are shown in Table IV. The reliabilities are higher for tests of the later pictures than for tests used for the first three pictures of the study, due partly at least to improvements in test construction. These tests were shorter for the second-third group than for the others during the 1929–30 portion of the study and possibly more difficult of comprehension. The reliabilities for this group therefore fluctuate from testing to testing more than do those of the other age-groups. All reliabilities for tests were obtained by correlating the odd- and even-numbered items and stepping up the obtained value by means of the Spearman-Brown prophecy formula. The factors which were mentioned as influencing the validity of the tests also affected their reliability, and in the light of this fact the reliabilities obtained are superior to what might have been expected in a study of this type.

Relationships existing between Specific and General tests.— At four points of the study, groups took the General and the Specific tests the same day. The correlations between the scores made on the two tests are high. Frequently, the correlation between the two tests is higher than the reliability of one of the tests, and in one instance it is greater than the reliability of either test. There is a definite relationship shown between the contents of the two types of tests since correlations between them are so uniform and are fairly high. Many of the items which were used for test construction could have been made into either general or specific test items.

Relationships between scores on motion-picture tests and age, mental age, reading age, and educational age.—At various times during the progress of the study, correlations were obtained between the scores on motion-picture tests and age, mental age, educational age, or reading age, which were

TABLE IV

RELIABILITIES OF TESTS USED IN THIS EXPERIMENT DURING 1929-31

TYPE OF TEST	GRADES 2–3		GRADES 5–6		GRADES 9–10		ADULT	
	Range	Median	Range	Median	Range	Median	Range	Median
General information:								
Pretest..........	.36–67	.56	.32–80	.60	.47–78	.60	.46–85	.62
General..........	.10–83	.75	.60–79	.64	.65–89	.70	.49–82	.69
1 and 1½ General..	.41–78	.66	.50–89	.75	.65–89	.75	.60–80	.68
2 General.........	.70–91	.90	.....	.....	.....	.....	.....	.....
Specific information:								
Specific.........	.50–89	.75	.79–95	.87	.77–95	.84	.56–97	.72
1 and 1½ Specific..	.21–85	.70	.73–91	.85	.63–96	.85	.66–97	.85
2 and 3 Specific..	.54–94	.76	.77–91	.87	.77–87	.82	.62–91	.87

This table should be read as follows: Reliabilities on tests of general information given to the second-third grade-group before seeing the pictures (Pretests) ranged from .36 to .67 with a median of .56, whereas the reliabilities of the same tests given to this age-group after seeing the pictures ranged from .10 to .83, the median being higher than the highest reliability made on the Pretests, and so on. The reliabilities of general-information tests were higher for groups which had seen the pictures than for groups which had not. Tests of specific information were more reliable than tests of general information.

obtained for the most part from school records. These correlations, of which more than 100 were computed, were quite low. Only two were more than .80, and most of them were but little above 0. In almost every case the correlation between a motion-picture test and age, mental age, or other measure was less than the reliability of the test. Jones found a high relationship between scores on tests of this type and Army Alpha, but his groups consisted of observers ranging in age from ten years to more than forty.[5] This range of talent would naturally cause a higher correlation between the two measures than would be the case if his group had been sectioned into two or three subgroups according to age, and these subgroups had been measured separately. The ability to remember the salient facts of a motion picture is a trait somewhat related to mental ability, reading ability, or general ability to learn, but the relationship is not strong.

Sectioning of questions according to kinds of action, types of action, and background.—The sectioning of this type which was carried out in 1929–30 has been described. During 1930–31, further refinements were effected. The 240 questions in the 6 tests of specific information were classified according to 10 kinds of action which occurred. These classifications were carefully defined beforehand, but definitions and examples of each kind of action were rather lengthy and will not be included. The kinds of action occurring in these pictures were emotion, crime, drinking, fighting, mystery, romance, sports, social activities, general conversation, and general action. The 7 types of action shown in these pictures were humorous, romantic, sad, strongly emotional, weakly emotional, neutral, and titles. The 12 kinds of background in which the action occurred were business, café, frontier,

[5] Conrad, Herbert S., and Jones, Harold Ellis, *Psychological Studies of Motion Pictures. III. Fidelity of Report as a Measure of Adult Intelligence.* University of California Publications in Psychology, 1918–1929 (1929, No. 7), 3, 245–276.

hotel, home, war, tenement, school, seas and ships, general exterior, outdoors, and titles.

Summary.—The group of motion pictures used in this experiment is considered a cross section of all pictures, this unitary aspect making it possible to combine the test data on all items of the same general type occurring in the various pictures. In each locality, each age-group was divided into three sections, equated on the basis of chronological age, mental age, and reading age. Each of the three administrations of each test was to a different section, and the results were regarded as though the same group had been given three equivalent tests at appropriate intervals. Statistical analyses of several types bore out the validity of this assumption. Yes-no (true-false), four-response and five-response multiple-choice, and completion questions, as well as brief themes, were used in testing motion-picture retention. The five-response multiple-choice question proved to be the type best adapted to the uses of the study. Various factors in the testing techniques employed interfered to produce second- and third-grade test scores which were higher than they should have been in respect to those of older observers. These factors were measurable to a certain extent, but they could not be corrected for with certainty. The methods used in analyzing earlier pictures and in constructing tests for them were retained with certain modifications. By the several methods used the tests were shown to be valid and reliable. The relationship was high between scores on general and specific tests, but low between scores on general or specific tests and chronological age, mental age, or educational age. The questions in the specific tests were classified according to the kind of action occurring at the time and according to the background in which the action occurred. Data from the results of these classifications will be presented in the following chapter.

CHAPTER III

RESULTS OF THE STUDY

The retention of specific information.—In order that this division of the study may not occupy too large a portion of the report, the statistical evaluations of data have been cut to the minimum. This is necessary in a discussion of the results obtained from over 20,000 tests given during nearly 700 testings in 11 communities of varying types. Reliabilities, probable errors of the measures, and other computations have been obtained, and where it is necessary to illustrate or emphasize a finding, these measures are reported. No reports of findings are given unless these findings are still present after a careful statistical analysis has been made and the data proved to be statistically significant.

The percentages of correct response on the various testings for each picture are shown in Table V. Mean scores for the first three pictures are omitted because of the difference between the construction of the tests for these pictures and those for later pictures.[1] Average scores are reported for the remaining pictures; the report is divided into two sections. The individual records of Pictures 11 to 16 are given in the upper part of the table. The total average scores on the pictures of 1929–30 (Pictures 4 to 10), seven in number, are given in the three last lines of the table, and are immediately preceded by the total average scores for the pictures of 1930–31 (Pictures 11 to 17). In these reports the average percentages of correct responses are given for each age-group on each testing of the specific-information tests.

[1] See Chapter II.

Table V

AVERAGE PERCENTAGES OF CORRECT RESPONSES, SPECIFIC TESTS
FOR PICTURES 4 TO 16

	Grades 2–3		Grades 5–6		Grades 9–10		Adults	
	Number	Average (Per Cent)	Number	Average (Per Cent)	Number	Average (Per Cent)	Number	Average (Per Cent)
11. "Tom Sawyer":								
Specific.	160	49.4	208	76.0	230	88.3	36	91.3
1½ Specific.	159	51.2	193	69.8	239	79.0	28	80.0
3 Specific.	163	55.0	172	67.1	225	74.6	33	70.4
12. "Passion Flower":								
Specific.	157	59.3	191	70.8	227	83.6	30	91.2
1½ Specific.	141	50.6	170	58.5	208	74.0	25	71.7
3 Specific.	94	46.9	136	57.4	186	68.8	25	80.0
13. "Gang Buster":								
Specific.	172	48.7	197	66.4	203	82.8	22	88.8
1½ Specific.	147	44.3	191	57.8	192	71.7	22	74.8
3 Specific.	47	40.7	65	61.7	112	60.3	25	75.7
14. "New Moon":								
Specific.	207	49.7	239	59.2	195	75.5	18	82.2
1½ Specific.	58	39.0	82	43.8	110	60.1	22	66.6
3 Specific.	45	35.9	63	38.7	102	52.9	26	67.1
15. "Fighting Caravans":								
Specific.	85	41.8	108	49.1	147	73.0	27	85.1
1½ Specific.	55	42.2	69	45.1	125	61.6	25	64.7
3 Specific.	48	40.9	61	42.5	107	57.1	..	......

Table V (Continued)

AVERAGE PERCENTAGES OF CORRECT RESPONSES, SPECIFIC TESTS FOR PICTURES 4 TO 16 (Continued)

	Grades 2-3		Grades 5-6		Grades 9-10		Adults	
	Number	Average (Per Cent)	Number	Average (Per Cent)	Number	Average (Per Cent)	Number	Average (Per Cent)
16. "Stolen Heaven":								
Specific..........	178	59.5	237	67.0	266	79.2	29	85.5
1½ Specific.........	52	50.2	84	62.1	143	69.0	.....	.....
3 Specific.........	29	51.0	27	63.8	106	65.6	.....	.....
Total Pictures 11 to 16 (1930–31):								
Specific.........	959	52.2	1,180	65.9	1,270	80.9	162	87.8
1½ Specific.........	612	47.4	789	58.8	1,017	71.0	122	71.8
3 Specific.........	426	47.8	524	56.2	838	65.4	109	73.0
Total Pictures 4 to 10 (1929–30):								
Specific.........	.....	52.8	.....	42.9	.....	53.5	.....	64.7
1 Specific.........	.....	56.7	.....	38.4	.....	42.2	.....	51.1
2 Specific.........	.....	51.1	.....	.....	.....	.....	.....	.....

This table may be interpreted as follows: The second-third grade-group answered the Specific test for "Tom Sawyer" 49.4 per cent correctly. A month and a half later an equated group from the same grades and schools answered the same questions 51.2 per cent correctly, a gain of 1.8 per cent of the total percentage or a gain of 3.6 per cent on the original responses. Three months after the picture was seen, a third equated group from the same grades answered the same test 55.0 per cent correctly, a gain of 5.6 per cent of the total or 11.3 per cent of the original responses, and so on.

The specific-information tests have been described in the previous chapters. Glancing through those brief descriptions or analyzing some of the specimen tests included in Appendix I one sees that a main factor in test construction was the preparation of a device for the measurement of reaction to and retention of a picture as a whole. Details were in themselves ignored; test questions which concerned small incidents in a picture were really intended to measure retention of that section of the picture which subtly hinged upon a seemingly minor portion. For example, consider the following item:

> 31. Felice said that when she was married she would be of help to her husband because she had (1) a wagon and horses (2) a lot of linen (3) some money (4) a number of furs (5) some furniture ("Fighting Caravans," Specific No. 31).

Her dowry was more or less immaterial, yet, if the entire situation is understood, this particular dowry becomes of decided importance. Clint, the prospective bridegroom, was a man of the plains, a frontiersman. Freedom meant more to him than any other thing, and the mention of linen had its implications of fixed residence and household duties. He suddenly fled in panic. While on his mad flight away from the caravan, he ran across evidence of the projected Indian attack and returned in time to organize the defense, thereby saving the lives of the members of the caravan. A considerable portion of the plot hinged upon Felice's innocent and apparently unimportant use of the word "linen." Although it might appear unimportant as a test question, in all probability it really tested the recall of a pertinent portion of the picture.

Radossawljewitsch, Ebbinghaus, and others have tested memory span over varying periods of time, and have found retention at the end of a month's time amounting to from 12 to 30 per cent. In this study retention at the end of a month was almost as high as in the original testing immediately after the picture; on occasions the average score of a group was even higher a month or more after than immediately following the picture (see Table V). The technique employed by Ballard is used here. The original retention (the day after the picture) is considered as 100 per cent in each case, and deviations are determined with this as the base.

During the 1930–31 study the time for the later testings was extended to one and one-half and three months, but even with this longer time and with a heterogeneous group of children there are still evidences of high retention. Reference to Table V will show that on "Tom Sawyer" and "Fighting Caravans" an increase occurred in the average scores of this age-group over even the longer interval of one and one-half months. One curious fact is that for "Tom Sawyer" there was still a further increase in the period between the 1½ Specific and 3 Specific tests. The retention of these children on the 1½ Specific was 104 per cent, and on the 3 Specific 111 per cent as high as their scores on the Specific. There was an increase from the 1½ Specific to the 3 Specific also on "Stolen Heaven," and at no point was the drop between these two testings at all large.

A brief analysis of Table VI will show several interesting changes in the percentages of correct responses from testing to testing of the individual items in the six specific tests of 1930–31. The six specific-information tests used in these years contained a total of 240 questions. Out of these a number were remembered better on the 1½ Specific or 3 Specific than on the Specific which followed the picture immediately. This factor of questions which were remembered better at a later day was found more frequently in the

tests of second-third grade-groups than in those of the older
groups. As an exception, however, it is to be noted that
nearly 60 per cent of the time the adults remembered situations better three months after the picture than they did a
month and a half after it. When the average scores on the
complete tests are considered, these increases are lost sight
of unless they occur in sufficient frequency to cause an entire
test average on a 1½ Specific or 3 Specific to surpass the average score for the same age-group on the Specific test.

This factor of retention is a major finding of the study and
is worthy of further analysis. It was previously thought that
children did not understand pictures, in the first place, and
did not remember them, in the second. It appears, however,
that children do understand pictures. What they see is present in their memories, practically intact, waiting only for a
stimulus to arouse it. They will probably never again meet
such a stimulus as the tests used in this experiment, but the
memories are there. A child goes to a picture for a variety
of reasons, but the content of the picture stays with him a
long time, without effort on his part. The factors which
cause this long-time retention, and even increase, will be
discussed in a later paragraph.

As shown in the second section of Table VI, there are
frequent questions on which the percentage of correct responses for one age-group is superior to that of an older age-
group, although, as shown in Table V, each age-group has a
total average percentage of correct responses which is larger
than that of each younger group. When the statistical technique involving the probable error of difference is used,
these superiorities are found to be in the main statistically
significant. Six of the 9 possible comparisons of age-groups
to those next younger show differences of 4 or more probable errors of difference and 2 more show differences of

TABLE VI

THE PERCENTAGES OF THE TWO HUNDRED FORTY QUESTIONS IN SIX SPECIFIC TESTS WHICH WERE ANSWERED BETTER ON LATER TESTINGS THAN ON EARLIER ONES, AND WHICH WERE ANSWERED BETTER BY YOUNGER OBSERVERS THAN BY OLDER ONES

	GRADES 2–3		GRADES 5–6		GRADES 9–10		ADULT [a]	
	Number of Cases	Per Cent of Items	Number of Cases	Per Cent of Items	Number of Cases	Per Cent of Items	Number of Cases	Per Cent of Items
Answers Better on Later than on Earlier Test								
Higher on the:								
1½ Specific than Specific..	86	35.8	56	23.3	26	10.8	41	20.5
3 Specific than Specific..	87	36.3	42	17.5	11	4.6	26	16.3
3 Specific than 1½ Specific	109	45.4	86	35.8	52	21.7	95	59.4
Answered Better by Younger than Older Observers								
Grades 5–6..............	51	21.3 [b]						
Grades 9–10.............	11	4.6 [b]	8	3.3				
Adults..................	7	2.9 [b]	8	3.3	45	18.8		

[a] Adults did not take one 1½ Specific and two 3 Specific tests; therefore comparisons involving 1½ and 3 Specific tests can be made on but 200 and 160 items, respectively.

[b] To be interpreted that the second-third grade-group was superior to the group indicated on the number of items and the percentage of the total number (240) as shown.

This table may be interpreted as follows: 35.8 per cent of the time second-third grade-group had higher average percentages of correct responses on the items of the 1½ Specific test than on the same items in Specific tests, and so on. This age-group had higher average scores on items in Specific tests 21.3 per cent of the time than did the fifth-sixth grade-group on these items, and so on.

3.25 *PE* and 3.90 *PE*, which give a high degree of reliability. When total tests are considered, each age-group has higher retention on specific tests than each younger age-group, but it is a different kind of retention. A young child has not the sense of values of an older child or an adult, and he seizes upon some inconsequential detail which has been ignored by the adults. Conversely, young children do not adequately comprehend the plot of a picture and do not grasp or do not remember certain important portions which register automatically with adults and older children. Retention of the material shown on the screen is tremendous for observers of all ages, and unconscious reorganization of data may lead to higher retention over longer periods of time than immediately following the viewing of the picture. This retention is in all probability almost entirely unconscious. It is the type of retention referred to in psychology as "non-voluntary" learning, which comes without conscious effort on the part of the observer.

A comparison of the retention of children from different localities.—It is difficult in the extreme to evaluate this factor within a short space. In the 1929–30 portion of the study variations between groups of the same age in different localities were not large. There was, however, but little variation in the communities available for the study. In 1930–31 a conscious effort was made to select communities which would yield as wide variations of modes of living and of family incomes as possible. In the list for that year was one of the select residential sections of Cincinnati, an average residential district in Columbus, the poorest district in Cincinnati, the small university town of Delaware, the small town of Wellsburg on the edge of the coal and iron district, and Jackson, a medium-sized city in the agricultural belt of the South. All types of occupations and all types of homes were represented. Taken together, this group forms a well-rounded cross section of American life. Taken separately, the communities provide a wealth of comparative data, worthy of a complete report in themselves.

In comparing the average scores of these six sections of each age-group the probable error of difference is used, and quotients are translated into chances in 100 of an actual superiority as indicated. If the mean score for one group is 45 and for another 53, and the probable error of difference is 2, then the difference between the scores, 8, divided by the probable error of the difference, 2, gives a quotient of 4. This shows a difference of 4 *PE* between the two means, which indicates less than one chance in 100 of the group having the average score of 45 actually being equal to the higher group in respect to the quality being tested.[2]

When the average score of each of the 6 sections of an age-group is compared to every other average score in the age-group, 15 comparisons are available. In order to illustrate the differences existing between the sections of each age-group, these 15 comparisons were made for each of the three age-groups on the average scores of the Specific test for "Passion Flower," making 45 comparisons in all. Sixteen of the 45 are larger than 4 *PE*, showing practical certainty of the superiority of certain sections over certain other sections. There are only 8 differences out of the total 45 which are less than 1 *PE*, a difference which might be expected solely by chance. All the extreme variations (4 *PE* or greater) occur in the second-third and fifth-sixth grade-groups.

[2] Garrett, H. E., *Statistics in Psychology and Education.* New York: Longmans, Green, 1926. Pp. xiii, 317.

Some of the communities showed definite superiorities over others of the group, yet there was no definite trend noticeable in this situation. Children in some of the localities, where living conditions were poor, showed a higher degree of retention than did other communities where conditions were more favorable. The relative standing of the groups of the same age from different localities were frequently reversed on other pictures. As far as this study could determine, none of this superiority of a group from one locality over a group of the same age from another locality could be attributed to the degree of frequency of movie attendance in either locality. Existing differences must have been due then to variations in environment which would cause children in one locality to notice actions and items of conversation or background which would pass unobserved with children of the same age in another locality.

There are two other methods of making this comparison. Each section of an age-group was compared in the same manner to the combined scores of the other sections of the age-groups, making 6 possible comparisons for each age-group, or 18 in all. Six of the 18 showed differences of 4 *PE* or more. These 6 were divided equally between the two youngest age-groups.

In the other method of comparison, the difference between the scores on the Specific test for "Passion Flower" for each pair of adjacent age-groups in each locality was measured in terms of the same yardstick—probable errors. These differences were then compared with the ones described in the earlier paragraphs of this section. For example, the difference between the average scores of the fifth-sixth grade-group and the second-third grade-group of Delaware was compared with the differences between the Delaware fifth-sixth grade and the other fifth-sixth grade-groups. The difference between the average score of each section for each age-group, and the adjacent age-group in the same community was compared to the difference between the section and the other five sections of the same age. As age-groups could be compared to younger ones as well as to older, four sets of comparisons were available, making a total of 120 comparisons. Out of these 120 comparisons, a total of 56, or nearly half, showed greater differences between children of the same grade but of different locality than between children two or more grades apart in the same locality. In other words, the average level of ability to understand and retain the material of this picture which was found in the second-third grade in one locality might not be found in another community until the fifth and sixth grades.

It is a difficult situation to understand. Intelligence, as measured by group tests, did not show a marked difference between localities, and ages were not significantly different. The variations in scores which occurred were frequently in favor of the younger children or children of lower mental or educational ability. The only conclusion which can be drawn is that at any given age or grade-level children from different localities do differ in their reactions to and retention of motion pictures. These variations are not the same for all pictures. Two groups of the same age in different localities may differ on the tests for one picture, and the direction of these differences may be reversed on tests for the next picture. Nor were these chance variations; they were statistically significant. A discussion of the material remembered best, or least, from the pictures may throw more light on this complex situation.

Retention of different kinds of action, types of action, and background.—When the study was initiated, one of the main objectives was an analysis of the factors producing differences in average test scores. If an age-group in a given locality does well on the tests for one picture and not so well on those for another, what factors have caused the change? Why does a group in one locality surpass a group of the same age in another locality in the retention of one picture and not of another? All tests which were used for the pictures were constructed on the basis of the same aims; they were made by the same group and carefully surveyed and revised before use. Several statistical check-ups showed that but few of these variations could be attributed to variations in the tests. These variations occurred as freely when Section A of an age-group was tested on two pictures as when Section A was tested on one and Section B on another. Here were definite variations in the types of things that children remembered, and the actual variations were therefore analyzed to ascertain the causes. If one picture contains a large proportion of romantic incidents which appeal to the children of a certain age in one community but which do not appeal to children of the same age in other communities, it may cause a higher retention of the picture on the part of the former group.

As mentioned in a previous chapter, all questions in the tests of specific information were divided according to the action taking place and also according to the type of action and the background in which the action occurred. These divisions were made carefully by a committee working from a set of written definitions. Ten main kinds of action were shown in the pictures of 1930–31 and from 9 to 51 questions were based on each. Table VII shows the rank of retention of each kind of action, based upon average percentages of retention, for each section at each age-level. There is a considerable variance in the average retention by the sections of each age-group. Sports are remembered best of all kinds of action by the second and third grades of two localities whereas in one locality sports rank next to last in average percentage of retention by this age-group. Definite tendencies are present, however. Sports, general action, and crime are usually remembered by all of the age-groups, while questions involving drinking, bootlegging, and business are not generally well retained.

Many of these data were not, however, statistically significant. When the probable errors of the difference were computed, many of the differences between average percentages of correct responses on two kinds of action when divided by the probable error gave quotients of less than 4 PE. This result was probably due to two factors: First, only 11 classifications were used, a situation which of necessity caused questions of fairly dissimilar type to be included within a single classification. Table VII covers data from 1930–31 only, and, as the classification of items varies slightly from that of the previous years, a combination of the data from the two periods is impossible at this point. Second, there were too few questions in several of the classifications, resulting in a large probable error of the mean for each of these classifications. The formula for the probable error of the mean is

$$PE_M = \frac{.6745\sigma_{\text{dis.}}}{\sqrt{\bar{N}}}$$

and when N, the number of questions in the category, is only 10 or 12, the probable error is large and the difference between the means of two classifications must needs be large to be statistically significant. If five or ten times as many pictures had been used in the experiment, the

TABLE VII

THE AVERAGE RETENTION OF EACH OF SEVERAL DIFFERENT KINDS OF ACTION BY CHILDREN AT EACH AGE-LEVEL IN EACH COMMUNITY ON TESTS OF SPECIFIC INFORMATION, 1930–31

COMMUNITY	KINDS OF ACTION										
	General Action	Crime	Sports	Romantic	Titles	Mystery	General Conversation	Fighting	Social Activities	Business	Drinking
Grades 2–3:											
Jackson (Rank)	2	3	1	6	5	4	10	7	8	9	11
Columbus	3	2	10	7	1	5	6	9	4	11	8
Wellsburg	1	2	6	5	9	8	7	3	10	4	11
Delaware	2	3	1	6	4	5	9	7	10	8	11
Cincinnati (Avondale)	4	1	7	5	6	9	3	2	8	11	10
Cincinnati (Raschig)	1	2	3	4	7	6	8	10	9	5	11
Total (Specific)	1	2	3	4	5	6	7	8	9	10	11
Total (1½ Specific)	2	3	4	5	1	8	9	7	11	6	10
Total (3 Specific)	2	3	4	6	1	8	9	5	11	7	10
Grades 5–6:											
Jackson (Rank)	2	3	1	5	4	7	9	8	5	10	11
Columbus	2	4	1	3	7	8	6	9	5	10	11
Wellsburg	2	3	1	4	8	5	6	7	10	9	11
Delaware	2	3	1	5	6	4	8	10	7	9	11
Cincinnati (Avondale)	2	3	1	4	7	9	6	8	10	5	11
Cincinnati (Raschig)	4	1	2	3	7	9	6	10	5	8	11
Total (Specific)	2	3	1	4	5	6	8	9	7	10	11
Total (1½ Specific)	2	3	1	5	4	6	10	9	7	8	11
Total (3 Specific)	1	3	4	5	2	6	10	8	9	7	11

TABLE VII (Continued)

THE AVERAGE RETENTION OF EACH OF SEVERAL DIFFERENT KINDS OF ACTION BY CHILDREN AT EACH AGE-LEVEL IN EACH COMMUNITY ON TESTS OF SPECIFIC INFORMATION, 1930-31

(Continued)

COMMUNITY	General Action	Crime	Sports	Romantic	Titles	Mystery	General Conversation	Fighting	Social Activities	Business	Drinking
Grades 9-10:											
Jackson (Rank)	2	4	1	5	6	3	8	9	7	10	11
Columbus	3	1	6	5	8	4	7	9	2	10	11
Wellsburg	2	6	1	4	5	3	8	9	10	7	11
Delaware	2	7	1	6	5	3	8	10	4	9	11
Cincinnati (Avondale)	4	9	1	5	6	3	8	10	2	7	11
Cincinnati (Raschig)	2	4	1	5	8	7	6	10	3	9	11
Total (Specific)	2	4	1	5	6	3	8	9	7	10	11
Total (1½ Specific)	1	4	2	6	3	5	9	10	8	7	11
Total (3 Specific)	2	5	3	6	1	4	10	9	8	7	11
Total Specific	2	5	1	3	10	4	6	7	8	9	11
Total 1½ Specific	1	3	5	4	7	2	9	8	10	6	11
Total 3 Specific	6	1	9	3	8	2	10	5	7	4	11
Number of questions in each category	15	31	13	51	12	9	47	19	15	12	16

This table may be read as follows: The second-third grade-group at Jackson remembered questions concerned with sports best and those concerned with drinking the least, whereas the same age-group at Columbus remembered questions concerned with titles best and those concerned with business the least, and so on.

chances of significant differences would have been materially increased.

There are, also, definite trends of forgetting for different kinds of action, which are likewise not statistically reliable if only the number of questions in each classification is taken into consideration, but which have a high reliability if the number of observers is considered. On the $1\frac{1}{2}$ Specific and 3 Specific tests drinking is still remembered the least. Sports are not, as a general rule, remembered so well over a longer period of time. The second-third grade-group retained items concerning titles and business better on the $1\frac{1}{2}$ Specific tests than on the Specific and those concerning titles, general action, and sports better on the 3 Specific than on the $1\frac{1}{2}$ Specific. The fifth-sixth grade-group retained several kinds of action better over a longer period of time than over a shorter, but the real surprise occurs in the adult group, which retained all kinds of action, except general action and sports, better on the 3 Specific than on the $1\frac{1}{2}$ Specific. Interesting variations also occur among the school children from community to community, but the amount of significance in these data does not warrant further analysis.

This large amount of retention of the content of motion pictures is not exclusive with any particular age-group, but it is common to all. Variations in retention from picture to picture seem to be closely linked with picture content; but it is impossible to say whether this is due to the action occurring during each picture, to the type of this action, or to the background in which it occurred. This problem presents a rich field for future investigation. Table VIII shows the rank order of retention of each type of action and of each kind of background. The types of action recognized in the pictures by the tests with the number of items in which each is referred to follow:

TYPE OF ACTION	NUMBER OF ITEMS
Humorous	95
Neutral	14
Romantic	16
Sad	9
Strongly emotional	56
Titles	12
Weakly emotional	38
Total	240

The kinds of backgrounds found in the pictures and the numbers of test items in which they were each referred to were:

KIND OF BACKGROUND	NUMBER OF ITEMS
Business establishment	21
Café	20
Frontier	23
General exterior	18
Home	40
Hotel	32
Outdoors	12
School	8
Seas and ships	20
Tenement	18
Titles	12
War	16
Total number	240

Since statistical significance is likewise lacking at this point, these data are given briefly and without a great deal of analysis. The items carrying an emotional appeal are more easily retained than those lacking it. There is no distinct tendency to retain items with any definite type of background, although the three classifications of "home," "school," and "tenement" are well retained. When items occur in a familiar type of surrounding, the action is more important than the background, and the items are well remembered.

Few definite conclusions can be drawn from the statistical analysis, however. Action which is understood or which occurs in familiar surroundings is much more likely to be retained than action which is little understood or which occurs in bizarre surroundings. When the surroundings are of a familiar type, they are ignored and attention is focused upon the action. Conversely, when surroundings are unusual in their character, they are attended to more closely, and a corresponding decrease occurs in attention to the action of the picture. Action of a highly emotional character is apparently of more importance to the plot of the picture than is that of a more subdued type, and consequently receives a richer store of attention from observers young and old.

Retention of plot as compared to retention of incident.—In a further analysis, all items of the last six pictures of 1929–30 were divided into two groups. One group contained questions concerning the plot of the picture, the action of the main characters, and other items indispensable to the story. The other contained items concerned with such things as clothing, backgrounds in which action occurred, and speech which served as amusement for the audience without advancing the plot of the picture. The test for "The Show of Shows" was omitted from this analysis, as that picture was in the form of a revue and had no predominant plot.

In the upper portion of Table IX, the average percentages of retention show that questions concerned with the plot of the picture have not only a more pronounced immediate

Table VIII

RANK ORDER OF RETENTION OF ITEMS COVERING DIFFERENT TYPES OF ACTION AND KINDS OF BACKGROUND IN SPECIFIC TESTS, 1930–31

Type of Action	Grades 2–3			Grades 5–6			Grades 9–10			Adults		
	Spe-cific	1½ Spe-cific	3 Spe-cific	Spe-cific	1½ Spe-cific	3 Spe-cific	Spe-cific	1½ Spe-cific	3 Spe-cific	Spe-cific	1½ Spe-cific	3 Spe-cific
Types of Action												
Sad	1	2.5	2	1	2	3	1	2	2	3	1	1
Weakly emotional	2	2.5	3	2	3	2	2	3	3	1	2.5	4
Strongly emotional	3	4	4	3	4	4	4	4	5	4	2.5	2
Titles	4	1	1	4	1	1	3	1	1	6	5	6
Humorous	5	5	5	5	5	6	6	6	6	5	6	7
Romantic	6	7	6	6	6	5	5	5	4	2	4	5
Neutral	7	6	7	7	7	7	7	7	7	7	7	3
Kinds of Background												
Tenement	1	2	3	4	6	6	4	6	5	3.5	7	1
Home	2	4	6	2	3	4	3	4	3	2	2.5	5
War	3	10	7	8.5	10	9	7	9	8	7	5	2
School	4	3	2	1	1	2	1	1	6	1	2.5	11
Hotel	5	11	8.5	8.5	7	7	8	8	7	6	12	4
Outdoors	6	6	4	5	5	5	9	5	4	12	8	6
General exterior	7	5	5	3	2	3	2	3	2	3.5	1	3
Business establishment	8	8.5	10	7	8	8	6	7	9	5	4	7
Titles	9	1	1	6	4	1	5	2	1	11	6	8
Seas and ships	10	7	11	10	9	10	12	12	11	10	9	10
Frontier	11	8.5	8.5	12	11	11	10	10.5	10	8	11	12
Café	12	12	12	11	12	12	11	10.5	12	9	10	9

retention, but are also retained better over a one-month period. The use of the probable error of the difference shows that these changes are statistically significant. The probable errors of the means are small, and the differences between the average scores on plot and incidental questions for an age-group show in every case but one at least 4 *PE* of difference. In each case, the difference between average percentages of correct responses on plot and incidental questions is greater for the 1 Specific than for the Specific.

In the 1930–31 data the same analysis has been made (see lower part of Table IX). In this analysis questions concerned with plot, but not essential to it, are segregated into an intermediate group. All age-groups made a higher average score on essential than on non-essential questions, and a higher average score on non-essential plot questions than on incidental questions (see Table IX). These differences increase for the 1½ Specific and increase still further for the 3 Specific. When questions are thus sectioned into three groups, the actual differences between means are smaller, and the differences divided by the probable error of the difference are also smaller, although only one is less than 1 *PE*, while several reached 4 *PE* in value. Differences between essential plot and incidental questions are all large, 10 of the 12 exceeding 4 *PE*. Most of these differences are significant. The chances that the types of questions numbered one, two, and three would accidentally have means in this relative order and show regular gradations in 12 comparisons of mean scores and 8 comparisons of percentages without a single exception are infinitely small. As the 1929–30 data are based partially upon completion questions, fewer observers were used, and the length of time between tests was shorter than for 1930–31, the two sets of data cannot be combined, but they tell the same story. Important por-

TABLE IX

AN ANALYSIS OF RETENTION OF ITEMS COVERING THE PLOT
OF THE PICTURE AND INCIDENTAL ITEMS

	MEAN PERCENTAGES OF ITEMS RETAINED			
	Grades 2–3	Grades 5–6	Grades 9–10	Adults
	Five Specific Tests, 1929–30			
Plot:				
Specific..........................	55.1	51.6	61.1	75.9
1 Specific....................	58.5	48.0	54.1	63.7
Incidental occurrences:				
Specific..........................	49.0	39.0	49.7	58.4
1 Specific........................	50.7	32.3	37.6	43.2
Retention ratio, plot................	106.2	93.0	88.5	83.9
Retention ratio, incidental..........	103.5	82.8	75.7	74.0
	Six Specific Tests, 1930–31			
1. Plot (essential):				
Specific..........................	53.3	68.6	83.6	90.7
1½ Specific.......................	49.6	62.9	72.4	77.3
3 Specific........................	48.6	60.4	70.3	79.7
2. Plot (non-essential):				
Specific..........................	49.8	65.0	80.8	86.5
1½ Specific.......................	44.3	54.7	66.8	71.7
3 Specific........................	42.8	51.6	60.7	74.5
3. Incidental occurrences:				
Specific..........................	48.4	55.2	71.4	80.8
1½ Specific.......................	40.8	41.4	54.4	59.1
3 Specific........................	39.4	38.7	48.4	60.3
Percentage 1½ Specific is of Specific:				
1. Plot (essential)................	93.1	91.7	86.6	85.2
2. Plot (non-essential)............	89.0	84.2	82.7	82.9
3. Incidental occurrences..........	84.3	75.0	76.2	73.1
Percentage 3 Specific is of Specific:				
1. Plot (essential)................	91.2	88.0	84.1	87.9
2. Plot (non-essential)............	85.9	79.4	75.1	86.1
3. Incidental occurrences..........	81.4	70.1	67.8	74.6

This table may be read as follows: The second-third grade-group taking the specific-information tests during 1929–30 retained items concerned with the plot of the picture 55.1 per cent correctly and incidental items 49.0 per cent correctly. On the 1 Specific tests this difference is still more pronounced, and so on.

tions of pictures are remembered better and longer than unimportant ones.[3]

This is neither an astonishing nor an unexpected discovery, but it is one which, in the light of the findings of the previous paragraph, needs to be discussed further. If portions of a picture are deemed important by the makers of the picture, it has been shown that by the process of giving these portions a high emotional tone they can be made to stand out. The important items, the items of a highly emotional type, are remembered better. Is this, however, always to the best interests of the observer? If pictures are constructed ideally and if they contain no incorrectly shown general information, this situation may be acceptable and even laudable. On the other hand, how can we be certain that any given picture is entirely free from propaganda and free from all accidental or premeditated distortion of actual fact? In a later paragraph it will be shown that there is a definite tendency to accept as true general information exhibited incorrectly on the screen. If an emotional scene—a scene of high importance in the plot of the picture—contains misinformation of a general character, this misinformation has great chances of being accepted as true. This statement is particularly true when young children view the picture.

Examples of questions coming in the classification used are:

Plot essential—Tanya came to the fort to   (1) make up with Michael   (2) laugh at Michael   (3) warn Michael   (4) get away from Boris   (5) <u>whip Michael</u>. ("New Moon," Specific, No. 30.)

(2) Plot non-essential—Joe's head was hurt by   (1) broken glass   (2) a policeman's club   (3) <u>a bullet</u>   (4) a rock   (5) a sharp knife. ("Stolen Heaven," Specific, No. 3.)

[3] However, it does not follow that unimportant or incidental items are badly remembered. Reference to Table IX shows that there is a high retention for all types of material, especially in the case of the younger children.

Incidental—Dulce said that her husband was like three kinds of (1) dogs (2) automobiles (3) <u>pianos</u> (4) radios (5) farms. ("Passion Flower," Specific, No. 1.)

The number of questions included in each classification were:

	GRADE 2–3	OLDER OBSERVERS
1929–30:		
Plot..................	92	174
Incidental..............	68	146
1930–31:		
Plot essential...........	128	128
Plot non-essential.......	60	60
Incidental..............	52	52

Comparison of retention of boys and girls.—As shown in Table X, there is little difference in the retention of masculine and feminine observers. Means are approximately equal, the variations present being so small that they might easily be due to chance. This is also true in respect to reliabilities of tests and reactions to questions on different kinds of action. This situation was so patent in the 1929–30 portion of the study that no mention was made of it in the 1930 report, although Porter discussed the matter briefly. She found that boys in the second and third grades had slightly higher retention on questions of revue and crime. The girls retained to a higher degree questions concerned with fighting, romance, and general action.[4] The one- or two-month periods were more than likely to swing the balance the other way. Total average scores for the two sexes were only 1 per cent apart.

[4] Porter, Elfa McWilliam, *The Curve of Retention in Moving Pictures for Young Children.* State University of Iowa, Unpublished Master's Thesis, 1930. Pp. 119.

Table X

AVERAGE PERCENTAGES OF CORRECT RESPONSES FOR BOYS
AND GIRLS ON TESTS OF SPECIFIC INFORMATION, 1930–31

	Grades 2–3		Grades 5–6		Grades 9–10		Adult	
	Number	Mean	Number	Mean	Number	Mean	Number	Mean
Specific:								
Boys.........	473	53.4	599	65.5	578	80.5	81	87.7
Girls.........	486	51.0	581	66.3	692	81.3	81	88.0
1½ Specific:								
Boys.........	289	49.3	409	59.5	488	71.0	80	71.8
Girls.........	323	45.6	380	58.0	529	71.1	42	71.7
3 Specific:								
Boys.........	199	50.7	262	56.0	366	64.9	46	76.0
Girls.........	227	45.2	262	56.4	472	65.8	63	70.9

The effect of motion pictures on general information.—One
of the primary purposes of this study was to determine the
amount and direction of change in general information which
was caused by motion pictures. There is, of course, a certain amount of general information to be gained from any
picture, yet some furnish it to a far larger degree than others.
This fact was especially important to this study. In order
to serve as a basis for the construction of test items, information in a picture must be reliable, objective, and of the proper
degree of difficulty.

By reliability of information is meant the probability
that a certain action or situation as shown by the movie
will in real life have the same outcome a large majority
of the time. This is not validity. In "Passion Flower"
a farm was a wedding gift, a perfectly valid transaction, yet
the unusualness of the gift made the information unreli-
able, as this type of wedding present cannot be expected
frequently. Action which has an emotional basis is also
largely unpredictable. Questions covering this type of ac-

tion are attitude questions, a type this study has attempted to avoid.

Questions for use in a study of this type must be so constructed that only one interpretation of the question can be made, and so worded that no portion of the question gives a hint as to the correct answer. Scoring must be so objective that a properly corrected paper will have the same score each time if given to a number of graders for correction. Questions must be easy enough for second-grade children yet difficult enough to be missed occasionally by members of the group of superior adults. Reliability of information and objectivity of tests can be controlled with a fair amount of ease, but the construction of items containing the proper degree of difficulty was a major problem.

If it is discovered that the misinformation occasionally shown in motion pictures is frequently accepted as the truth, an important discovery has been made. In "The Mysterious Island" there were a number of incidents of a rather fantastic nature which were contrary to the scientific facts of to-day. A submarine went to the bottom of the ocean at a depth of two miles; the occupants donned diving suits, explored, and found a race of undersea people, a huge animal resembling the old dinosaur stegosaurus, and so on. Half of the questions in the test for older observers were based upon incorrectly shown action of this type, and the remaining twenty based upon correctly shown items. Table XI shows the average percentages of correct responses for the two types of questions on each administration of the test, in which 17 items were shown contrary to fact and 13 items shown correctly, each with 20 other items. All groups show higher percentages of increase on the General over the Pretest for correctly shown items as compared to incorrectly shown items. Children in the second-third grade-group apparently pay less attention to inconsistencies, or understand them less, and are less influenced by them. This analysis shows a distinct influence of motion pictures upon general information.

TABLE XI

A COMPARISON OF PERCENTAGES OF CORRECT RESPONSES ON ITEMS SHOWN CORRECTLY AND ITEMS SHOWN INCORRECTLY IN "THE MYSTERIOUS ISLAND," GENERAL–INFORMATION TESTS

TEST	PERCENTAGES OF CORRECT RESPONSE			
	Grades 2–3	Grades 5–6	Grades 9–10	Adult
	Items Shown Contrary to Fact			
Pretest	30.6	29.4	34.1	36.7
General	42.1	36.7	39.8	38.5
1 General	40.0	30.0	36.5	40.4
2 General	42.8	....	....	....
	Items Shown True to Fact			
Pretest	30.8	32.3	49.0	67.7
General	50.2	61.0	66.4	69.7
1 General	54.6	53.3	60.4	73.1
2 General	60.9	....	....	....

This table may be read as follows: The second-third group had approximately equal scores on correctly and incorrectly shown items in the Pretest, but on the General test given the day following the picture, the average percentages of correct responses were considerably higher on the correctly shown items, and so on.

During 1930–31 this factor was taken more carefully into account. Two pictures in particular offered a considerable amount of general information which was far from the truth, as well as it could be determined by careful investigation. In "New Moon" a Russian second lieutenant, a post filled from the peasant class, falls in love with and marries a princess whose uncle (father's brother) is only a count. The second lieutenant is in charge of a company of soldiers and later in charge of an important frontier fortress. Numerous geographical data are wrong as are even some of the physical data, such as the sending of a telegram from the Caspian Sea to Petrograd and the almost instantaneous receipt of the answer. This is a practically impossible accomplishment in present-day America, and is even more so in Russia. In "Fighting Caravans" a tank car of kerosene was hauled by wagon train across the prairies in 1861, whereas kerosene only became something more than a scientific curiosity late in that decade with the advent of the kerosene lamp. It is just as important, if not more so, to determine the reactions of observers to items incorrectly shown as it is to find out how their fund of general information has been increased by correctly shown items. If an item is shown correctly and the percentages of correct responses on that item increase after the picture is seen, there is, at least, partial proof that the picture has had an influence, while if an item is shown incorrectly and the percentages of correct responses decrease appreciably, the corroborating evidence is strong. To make matters doubly sure concerning the reactions to these two types of questions, there was inserted in each of the last three general tests a set of 5 items of exactly the same type as those of the regular test and covering the same subject-matter, but concerned with information not shown in the picture. The observers' reaction to these items was unusual. Presumably, they were puzzled by their inability to answer these items from what they had seen in the picture, and cast around for possible answers from this source. Consequently, there was a higher percentage of these items not answered on the General tests, and the percentages of correct response declined slightly (see Table XII). Items shown incorrectly had considerably lower percentages of correct response on the General tests than on the Pretests.

TABLE XII

AVERAGE PERCENTAGES OF CORRECT RESPONSES—TOTAL OF ALL GENERAL TESTS, 1930–31

TYPES OF ITEMS	GRADES 2–3	GRADES 5–6	GRADES 9–10	ADULTS
Shown correctly:				
Pretest	37.7	36.1	47.8	61.0
General	42.2	47.2	64.0	78.2
1½ General	42.7	44.1	60.9	71.6
Shown incorrectly:				
Pretest	34.9	31.4	41.7	53.0
General	32.2	25.4	27.6	33.1
1½ General	28.7	25.2	34.2	42.2
Not shown:				
Pretest	36.5	30.9	45.6	61.1
General	33.3	31.4	38.5	53.6
1½ General	34.5	33.6	43.0	55.8
	Percentage of the Pretest			
Shown correctly:				
General	111.9	130.7	133.9	128.2
1½ General	113.3	122.2	127.4	117.4
Shown incorrectly:				
General	92.3	80.9	66.2	62.5
1½ General	82.2	80.3	82.0	79.6
Not shown:				
General	91.2	101.6	84.4	87.7
1½ General	94.5	108.7	94.3	91.3

This table may be read as follows: The second-third grade-group increased its average scores on items shown correctly 12 per cent between the Pretests and the General tests. That is, their general information concerning the topics shown in the pictures increased on the average 12 per cent by seeing the picture if the items were shown correctly. If the items were shown incorrectly, seeing the picture decreased their general information 8 per cent, and so on.

One other point should be discussed in connection with differences in response to correctly and incorrectly shown items. In the case of "The Mysterious Island" the mean score on items shown incorrectly rose slightly on the General as compared to the Pretest, although for none of the school groups did the rise even approximate that of the mean score of items shown correctly. This rise is easily explained when the character of the picture is taken into account. "The Mysterious Island" is much like a fairy tale; the incongruities in it are so absurd that most people immediately recognize them as fallacious. Therefore, in only a few cases was there an actual decrease in means of incorrectly shown items.

This paragraph joins closely to those covering specific information. The two types of information should really be discussed simultaneously, as the section of a picture from which a specific-information item is taken frequently yields an additional item covering general information. It has been noted that for all ages of observers, but particularly for children of the second and third grades, items of specific information in pictures are sometimes retained better over a longer period of time than over a shorter. This is also true of items of general information. There are cases in which an item of this type has a higher percentage of correct responses on the $1\frac{1}{2}$ General test than on the General test immediately following the picture. Reorganization of the plot of the picture apparently aids retention of the general information contained in the picture.

Summary.—The retention of specific information from motion pictures is high. The retention of second-third grade and older children was 59 per cent or more of that of superior adults. Retention over a period of a month and a half averaged 90 per cent of the amount retained the day after the picture for the three groups of school children and 82 per cent for the adults. On many of the items the retention of a younger group was higher than that of one or more older groups. Sometimes items, or even whole tests, were retained better for a grade-group over a longer period of time than over a shorter. Children in the same grade-groups in different localities varied considerably in their retention of the pictures. A superiority of one locality over another on one picture was frequently reversed in the tests for another picture.

In general, action was remembered best when it concerned items of sports, general action, and crime, when it was somewhat emotional and when it occurred in a familiar type of background, such as home or school. Business, bootlegging, and drinking were not remembered well, nor were items with little emotional appeal nor items occurring in unfamiliar and interesting settings which would attract attention away from the action occurring at the time. Items of major interest to the plot of the story were retained over a short time much better than were incidental items; this superiority increased over a longer period of time. There was little difference in the retention of boys and girls. General information presented by the pictures was retained to a large extent if it was shown correctly in the pictures. These increases ranged from 12 per cent to 34 per cent for the different age-groups. Information shown incorrectly in the pictures was largely accepted. These decreases in general information ranged from 8 per cent to 38 per cent.

CHAPTER IV

A COMPARISON OF THIS STUDY AND OTHER STUDIES IN LEARNING

A comparison of this study and earlier studies of learning.— The various phases of memory have long constituted a fruitful field for speculation and theorizing. Some of the scientific approaches were completed over forty-five years ago—those of Ebbinghaus during 1879–85—but still have a considerable amount to contribute to the present-day discussions of the problem.

Ebbinghaus has carried out the pioneer, and probably the outstanding, research in memory. Using nonsense syllables largely, he tested other observers and himself to determine the character of retention over various lengths of time and under different conditions. His experiments included the introduction of new sets to be learned between the original learning and the recall, the relearning, the amount lost being indicated by the time or the number of repetitions necessary to bring the learning back to its former degree of excellency. His experiments were carried out under laboratory conditions, and his material to be memorized consisted largely of meaningless or uninteresting material.[1]

Since then, Müller, Schumann, Meumann, Radossawlje-witsch, and others worked out experiments of a similar nature, improving the techniques of Ebbinghaus. Two methods of testing the efficiency of the memory are in general use: the method of correct associates and the saving method. The

[1] Ebbinghaus, H., *Über das Gedachtnis* (translated by Ruger and Bussenius). New York: Teach. Coll., Columbia Univ., 1913. Pp. 123.

former is used to test organization; that is, parts of the learned material are furnished as stimuli and the omitted parts are to be furnished by the observer. In the saving method the amount of practice necessary to relearn the material forgotten during the interim is the measure of the amount retained. This study used the method of correct associates.

Ballard used the students in 42 senior departments of the elementary schools of London in his experiment in the memorization of poetry. He supplied each student with a copy of a 34-line selection which had been read to each class, had it studied briefly, and then asked each pupil to write all he could remember of what he had learned. Ballard divided the 42 departments into 7 equated groups and unexpectedly asked each of the separate groups for repetitions of the writing at periods varying from one to seven days after the original memorization. This procedure was followed in the memorization of several poems, a nonsense verse, diagrams, and the like. In each case, if the amount recalled immediately after the memorization was considered as 100 per cent, the change from this original basis was in the direction of increased retention over periods of one to six days, varying with the type of material learned, the age, sex, intelligence, and experience of the learner. Ballard notes especially the fact that much that was originally learned was forgotten during this period, so that this apparent superiority of the second test over the first really represents an actual superiority plus additional material to make up for that lost. He refers to this new material, the result of the process of maturation, as "reminiscence," which he states may be due to removal of obstructing inhibitions, removal of fatigue due to memorizing, or other causes.[2] Ballard is one of the few

[2] Ballard, P. B., *Obliviscence and Reminiscence.* Brit. J. Psychol. Monog. Suppl. 1913, 1, No. 2.   Pp. vii, 82.

who have discovered this maturation effect and noted more than casual interest in it as a portion of a learning experiment. His study is probably closer to this experiment than any of the others reviewed here.

The findings of Ballard's study have been borne out by this one. The authors of this report hesitate to use the word "reminiscence," yet the same condition prevails here as with Ballard. In the case of the retention of earlier pictures by the second-third grade-group and even by older observers, there were found pictures for which the average scores were lower on the Specific or General test administered the day following the picture than were the scores on the same test given to equated groups a month later. This increase was not an increase on all items included in the test. On many items the retention decreased, yet on the rest of the items there was a sufficient increase to more than compensate for the deficiency. Some of this situation shows itself in Table VI.[3]

In all of these experiments there is an emphasis upon the formal technicalities of memorization. The material to be learned is carefully standardized and given to the subject in an exact way. He is usually uninterested in the content, or he carries as a secondary interest in it a wish to please a professor, to pass the course, or to earn the promised sum of money for the time spent. As a usual thing, only the material to be recalled is memorized at the time, although confusion material may be memorized in the interim before recall is requested. Practice is carried forward in most of these experiments until learning is complete, but the mechanical nature of the material memorized causes rather quick forgetting.

In the organization of this problem only one view of the

[3] See page 43.

picture was presented. The pupils saw the entire picture without knowledge of the sections which would be asked in recall, and were present at the show with the attitude of seeking enjoyment rather than of attempting to memorize. Periods of testing were stretched to three months and in one case seven months after the show. Under these conditions results should, and do, differ markedly from those of Ebbinghaus, Meumann, and others.

The percentages of retention over a period of one day as obtained by Radossawljewitsch and by this study are not capable of exact comparison. In the former studies, retention was based upon material which was repeated until learning was just complete, and the percentages given indicate retention of this perfectly learned material. In this study, the children saw each picture once only. Much confusion material, that is, items not covered by test items, was present, including several reels of comedy and news in addition to the feature, and much of this confusion material was indistinguishable from the material to be tested. When these points are understood, it is not peculiar that the one-day testings of the two studies show different results. The real comparison between the two studies lies in the lower section of Table XIII where percentages of long-time retention are based upon one-day retention. The retention found by this study is far higher over a long period of time than is that found by former experimenters.

Experiments with motion pictures.—Psychological experiments using motion pictures have been few. There have been a number of studies in the usefulness of movies for the purpose of visual instruction, which will not be reviewed here as they are fairly numerous, similar in type, and far from the present study in method and aim. Jones has completed probably the only study which merits description.

He worked with eight villages in Vermont, using the ordinary audiences which were attracted by free movies. Immediately after the show he turned on the lights and tested retention by the use of multiple-choice and completion questions. His results showed that the curve of retention increased from the age of ten, the lowest age included in the study, to adulthood and declined somewhat after the age of forty.[4] In another section of the study he attempted to determine the efficiency of motion-picture tests as measures of intelligence, finding correlation coefficients with Army Alpha of .621 to .712 with small probable errors.[5]

Mitchell made an analysis of the movie attendance of 10,052 Chicago children of three types, delinquents in detention homes, normal children, and Boy and Girl Scouts. She attempted to analyze the motives which led to movie attendance and drew inferences from the records of movie attendance and types and ages of children. Throughout her book, she emphasizes the strong relationship of delinquency and frequent attendance at motion pictures. She says:

> The extent to which a child is exposed to the movies is in direct proportion to certain factors that enter his life. Delinquent children attend the movies more frequently than do other children. Scouts go to the movies less frequently than do other children, but they go regularly. The only difference between the movie attendance of a child who has directed interests in his life and the child whose recreation is left to his own guidance is in degree.[6]

[4] Jones, Harold Ellis, Conrad, Herbert, and Horn, Aaron, *Psychological Studies of Motion Pictures. II: Observation and Recall as a Function of Age.* University of California Publications in Psychology, 1918–1929 (1928 No. 6), 3, 225–243.

[5] Conrad, Herbert S., and Jones, Harold Ellis, *Psychological Studies of Motion Pictures. III: Fidelity of Report as a Measure of Adult Intelligence.* University of California Publications in Psychology, 1918–1929 (1929 No. 7), 3, 245–276.

[6] Mitchell, Alice Miller, *Children and Movies.* Chicago: Univ. Chicago Press, 1929. Pp. xxiv, 181. (P. 28.)

Table XIII

A COMPARISON OF THE RETENTION OF MEANINGFUL MATE-
RIAL FOUND IN THE EXPERIMENTS OF RADOSSAWLJE-
WITSCH AND OF THAT FOUND IN THESE
EXPERIMENTS

Experiment	Spe-cific	1 Spe-cific	1½ Spe-cific	3 Spe-cific	7 Spe-cific
	Percentages of Retention				
Radossawljewitsch:					
Children	79.0	24.3	....	....	....
Adults	79.7	23.9	....	....	....
Six Specific Tests:					
Grades 2-3	52.2	....	47.4	47.8	....
Grades 5-6	65.9	....	58.8	56.2	....
Grades 9-10	80.9	....	71.0	65.4	....
Adult	87.8	....	71.8	73.0	....
"Why Bring That Up?" [a]					
Grades 2-3	49.4	50.4	....	....	46.8
Grades 5-6	47.5	37.1	....	....	33.9
Grades 9-10	56.5	45.1	....	....	32.2
Adult	66.8	49.3	....	....	45.0
	Percentages of Retention, Considering the Amount Retained One Day as 100 Per Cent				
Radossawljewitsch:					
Children	....	30.8	....	....	....
Adults	....	30.0	....	....	....
Six Specific Tests:					
Grades 2-3	....	....	90.8	91.6	....
Grades 5-6	....	....	89.2	85.3	....
Grades 9-10	....	....	87.8	80.8	....
Adult	....	....	81.8	83.1	....
"Why Bring That Up?"					
Grades 2-3	....	102.0	....	....	94.7
Grades 5-6	....	78.1	....	....	71.4
Grades 9-10	....	79.9	....	....	57.0
Adult	....	74.0	....	....	67.4

[a] Tests for this picture were repeated seven months after the picture, with the results given in this table.

This table may be interpreted as follows: In the experiments of Radossawl-jewitsch, retention over a month's time amounted to but 30 per cent of the amount retained the day following the original learning. In this experiment, retention of a similar character amounted to from 82 per cent to 91 per cent over the period of a month and a half, and so on.

The majority of children come in contact with the movies once or twice a week. Any institution that touches the life of a child with this persistent regularity becomes of high importance to his welfare. Delinquent children attend movies more often than other children, go more frequently at night, and attend without their parents a larger percentage of the time. However, in her concluding paragraph she states,

> The delinquent child's extensive contact with the movie may or may not be due to the fact that he is a delinquent and because of the things back of his delinquency. Whether or not the movie enters into his delinquency is a subject for further research and is out of the realm of this study. The present data only show that the delinquent does have a wider movie experience than do the other children studied.[7]

The present investigation is part of the first real attempt at the evaluation of the effect of motion pictures. Porter working in conjunction with the authors arrived at several interesting conclusions with regard to the memory of primary-school children upon attending movies. These were discussed in conjunction with the results of this study.[8]

The possible utilization of these findings by several fields related to educational psychology.—These findings will naturally be of more interest to educational psychologists than to the students of any other field of knowledge, as the experiment is concerned primarily with phases of the learning problem. There are, however, various related fields which borrow generously from educational psychology, and the contribution of this study to each of these fields is given here briefly.

1. Education.—The use of slides, stereopticans, and motion pictures in visual education has been increasing rapidly

[7] *Op. cit.*, p. 142.
[8] Porter, Elfa McWilliam, *The Curve of Retention in Moving Pictures for Young Children.* State University of Iowa, Unpublished Master's Thesis, 1930. Pp. 119.

in the past decade. This study was not concerned with educational pictures, yet the fact that tremendous retention of scenes and action from ordinary motion pictures was found may lead to an increased use of motion pictures as teaching devices. The retention found here would probably not be duplicated in strictly educational pictures, yet the added incentive present in the classroom, the possibility of reshowing of pictures, and the careful description of each action as it occurs in the educational picture might compensate for the difference between the educational film and the one used for entertainment only. Many pictures marketed for their entertainment value possess tremendous possibilities from a purely educational standpoint. Such pictures as "Simba," "Rango," "Chang," "Nanook of the North," "With Byrd at the South Pole," "The Four Feathers," and others have better teaching possibilities than hours of study on geography lessons. Such pictures as "Abraham Lincoln," "Scaramouche," "The Birth of a Nation," and "The Ten Commandments" present historical facts in a clear and easily understood manner although incorrect action is frequently introduced.

Many of our present-day trends in speech, clothing, and house furnishings are directly attributable to motion pictures. Pictures contribute a considerable amount to our scientific information, but much of this contribution is fallacious and, therefore, worse than useless. Some of the pictures produced for entertainment purposes could legitimately be transported into the schoolroom and used as teaching devices.

2. Child welfare.—Various organized groups of interested persons make monthly reports of pictures recommended for children. Certain pictures are not recommended because of items deemed by the reviewer to be undesirable and harm-

ful. The findings of this study as to the kinds and types of action best and least remembered and the amounts of retention of both specific and general information might well assist in placing these reviews on a reliable basis. Those who review motion pictures for censorship boards or for various social-service agencies might be interested in the findings of this study for the same reason.

The possible effect of these findings on motion pictures.— If these findings are utilized by the motion-picture industry, two results will occur: First, the pictures will be more carefully scrutinized for incongruities and misinformation. One of the chief duties of assistant directors is to make certain of the authenticity of all portions of pictures, yet this duty is frequently slighted. Various items of misinformation are occasionally necessary, but as far as possible these should be so shown that their lack of validity is quite apparent. Second, many pictures prepared for regular theater showings might well be exhibited as regular classroom work. A closer coöperation between producers and educators would be necessary to bring about this innovation.

Summary.—The findings of the study have possible value in their contribution to the general field of learning and retention, as the percentages here obtained were considerably higher than those obtained by previous investigators in the field of retention. Motion pictures appear to have more of a possible contribution to visual education than was previously suspected. Many pictures made for their power to attract box-office receipts have real value in the fields of English, history, and geography. The findings of this study may be of benefit to various boards of motion-picture review. There is at present a real opportunity for producers to show selected pictures in school for the sake of their educational value as well as their entertainment.

CHAPTER V

SUMMARY AND CONCLUSIONS

A brief review of testing techniques.—This study has been carried out with two principal aims in view: to measure the amount and types of information concerning the specific action and background of selected motion pictures which are retained over periods ranging from one day to three months, and to measure the amount and types of general information received from selected motion pictures which are retained over periods ranging from one day to a month and a half. Seventeen pictures were used in the study. For each of these, with one exception, a specific-information test was constructed and given to a third of the observers a day after the exhibition of the picture, was repeated for another third a month or a month and a half later, and for the remaining third was repeated two or three months later. The three groups of observers were equated on the basis of age, mental age, educational age, and all other available measurements. Observers were obtained from the second and third grades, the fifth and sixth grades, the ninth and tenth grades, and superior adults. The second-third grade-group was tested with abbreviated forms of the tests used for older observers.

The same groups were used for tests of general information. Each test was given as a Pretest before the picture to one group; it was given to another group the day following the picture; and it was repeated with the third group a month or a month and a half later. For tests of both types of information the groups were rotated, Group A taking the specific-information test for one picture the day after the exhibition, for the next picture a month and a half after the exhibition, and for the next picture three months after the exhibition.

Nearly 3,000 observers have assisted for one or more tests. There were in all 26 tests consisting of from 30 to 64 items each administered in the aggregate for more than 20,000 testings. A total of over 813,000 items was attempted.

Conclusions drawn from the data of preceding chapters.— Several assumptions concerning equating of groups, combination of data from tests of several pictures, and other techniques were made at the beginning of the study, but all were proved empirically during the progress of the study. The tests used were entirely objective; they made satisfactory provision for an extreme range of talent and were reliable and valid. All statistical procedures necessary to determine these facts and also the conclusions of the following paragraphs have been computed. The following conclusions may therefore be drawn from the data which have been presented:

1. The general information of children and adults is increased to a considerable extent by correctly shown information from motion pictures. On the tests of general information used in this study, the average scores of the groups from the second and third grades, the fifth and sixth grades, the ninth and tenth grades, and the superior adults increased 11.9 per cent, 30.7 per cent, 33.9 per cent, and 28.2 per cent, respectively. This [retention is lasting, the percentages of increase between the Pretest and the same test given a month and a half after the exhibition being nearly as large as those obtained the day after the picture.]

2. General information presented incorrectly by the pictures is frequently accepted as valid unless the incongruity is quite apparent. For the four age-groups, decreases in average scores on the general-information tests amounted to 7.7 per cent, 19.1 per cent, 33.8 per cent, and 37.5 per cent, respectively, when information was shown incorrectly. These decreases were relatively lasting, even increasing for the two youngest age-groups and decreasing somewhat for the two older age-groups. The content of a picture is accepted as authentic by a large percentage of the audience unless the errors contained are glaring.

3. Retention of the specific incidents of motion pictures is high. Children, even very young ones, can retain specific memories of a picture with a high degree of accuracy and completeness. The second-third grade-group retained on the average nearly 60 per cent as much as the group of superior adults. This retention of scenes from motion pictures is high over a long period of time. A third of each age-group was not tested for three months after each picture, yet the average scores for these groups were 91.6 per cent, 85.3 per cent, 80.8 per cent, and 83.1 per cent as high, respectively, for the second and third grades, the fifth and sixth grades, the ninth and tenth grades, and the adults as they were for equated groups at each age-level the day after the picture. On many individual items the average percentage of correct responses of a younger age-group was higher than that of one or more older age-groups.

4. On some individual test items and occasionally on entire tests, an age-group had a higher average retention on tests a month and a half or three months after the picture than it did the day after the picture. This situation occurred most frequently in the second and third grades, but it was common with all three of the older groups. Although a

picture may seem to fade from consciousness quite rapidly, when the proper stimulus (the test) is used the retention is remarkably high, and because of a settling out of unimportant details it may be remembered even better than at first.

5. Action was remembered best when it concerned activities such as sports, general action, crime, and fighting; when it had a high emotional appeal; and when it occurred in a familiar type of surrounding, such as home, school, or tenement. Action was understood least when it concerned unfamiliar activities such as bootlegging and business; when it had practically no emotional elements; and when it occurred in surroundings of an unfamiliar and interesting type, such as café and frontier.

6. Portions of the picture which were concerned directly with the plot of the story were remembered better by all age-groups the day after the picture than were items concerned with incidental details such as clothes, background, and casual speeches. This superiority increased over the period of a month and a half, and it increased still further on the tests three months after the exhibitions. The important items were remembered better initially; this superiority increased with the passage of time.

7. There was little or no difference in the retention of boys and girls in this study.

8. These high retentions occur with children in a detention home as well as with normal children.

9. The percentages of retention found by this study surpass to a large degree the percentages previously obtained from learning experiments. This is true in spite of the fact that in this experiment the incentive to learn was absent; the material to be learned was not even identified amid the mass of confusion items; and there was but one exhibition

of each picture which occurred in a noisy theater filled with friends of the observers. Each of these points is in direct contrast to the elaborate procedures in use in other experiments in learning.

10. Certain of these findings may prove to be of value to the fields of education and child welfare, and to the motion-picture industry itself.

APPENDIX I

SAMPLES OF TESTS

"NEW MOON"

A SPECIFIC TEST

The following sentences describe some of the action or setting of the movie. In each sentence select the answer which you think is correct or which comes closest to being the correct one. Notice its number and put a cross in the circle which has the same number as the correct answer. Here is a sample, not taken from the movie.

The capital of Ohio is (1) Dayton (2) Cincinnati (3) Cleveland (4) Columbus (5) Toledo.

1( )   2( )   3( )   4(×)   5( )

In this case, Columbus, number 4, is the correct answer, so there is a cross in circle 4. *Mark only one answer for each question.*

Do not hurry. These answers do not affect your school grades; we just want to find out what you liked about the movie as shown by what you remember about it.

If you forget who was who in the picture, look at this list.

> Michael—the lieutenant
> Tanya—the princess
> Boris—the governor
> Igor—the count
> Potkin—the orderly

1. The actor who played the lead in this picture was (1) John Boles (2) Ramon Navarro (3) Ronald Colman (4) Dennis King (5) Lawrence Tibbett.   1( )   2( )   3( )   4( )   5( )

2. Potkin gave the peasant girl (1) a cigarette (2) a cookie (3) a parrot (4) a bracelet (5) an apple.

1( )   2( )   3( )   4( )   5( )

3. When the princess watched the people on the lower deck, Michael said he thought she might be angry because (1) he had his coat off (2) he had his arm around a peasant girl (3) he was amusing the

peasants (4) he had not noticed her before (5) he was eating an apple. 1( ) 2( ) 3( ) 4( ) 5( )

4. Potkin, the orderly for Michael, was hurt several times when (1) he fell out of his bunk (2) he hit the back of his head on a window (3) he slipped and fell down (4) his chair tipped over backwards (5) Michael knocked him down.
1( ) 2( ) 3( ) 4( ) 5( )

5. When the princess asked Michael to sing the gypsy song in English, he (1) sang it with the right English words (2) sang it with some other English words (3) refused to sing it (4) sang it in gypsy words (5) played it on the piano.
1( ) 2( ) 3( ) 4( ) 5( )

6. When the princess asked Michael to translate the song for her, he said, (1) "It is a 'naughty' song" (2) "I don't know what it means" (3) "Some of the words are not in our language" (4) "I have forgotten it" (5) "I have to leave now."
1( ) 2( ) 3( ) 4( ) 5( )

7. When Michael said he had almost forgotten she was a princess, Tanya replied, (1) "What can I do to help you forget?" (2) "You should never forget" (3) "I am not a princess to you" (4) "*I* cannot forget" (5) "A soldier should know better."
1( ) 2( ) 3( ) 4( ) 5( )

8. When the uncle saw Michael in the princess' room, he (1) told him to leave before anyone saw him (2) told his wife that everything was all right (3) sent for the captain (4) told his wife to go to the princess' room (5) told Tanya to send Michael away.
1( ) 2( ) 3( ) 4( ) 5( )

9. On the deck the last night on board, Tanya said that it was fun (1) fooling the people on board (2) singing for the people (3) pretending she did not love Michael (4) throwing away Michael's cigarettes (5) getting to Krasnov.
1( ) 2( ) 3( ) 4( ) 5( )

10. When the people on the boat asked the princess to sing, she and Michael sang (1) "I Love You Truly" (2) "Venetian Love Song" (3) "One Alone" (4) "Wanting You" (5) "Volga Boat Song."
1( ) 2( ) 3( ) 4( ) 5( )

11. The princess refused to sing more than one song because (1) she did not like the people who asked her (2) she wanted to be with Michael (3) she was tired and wanted to sleep (4) her aunt told her to leave (5) she did not want to stay with Michael.
1( ) 2( ) 3( ) 4( ) 5( )

12. The countess said that the count had married her because (1) he loved her (2) she had a lot of money (3) she was beautiful (4) her father was a nobleman (5) he thought she was rich.

    1( )   2( )   3( )   4( )   5( )

13. The countess knew that her husband was hiding something from her since (1) he drank so much (2) he laughed too much (3) he called her "baby" (4) he could not keep his mind on the cards (5) he wanted to go for a walk on deck.

    1( )   2( )   3( )   4( )   5( )

14. Boris gave the soldiers forty-eight hours leave in honor of (1) his recent election as governor (2) their successful voyage (3) his engagement to Tanya (4) their bravery in fighting (5) the Emperor's birthday.   1( )   2( )   3( )   4( )   5( )

15. One of the songs which is sung in this picture is (1) "Russian Lullaby" (2) "Love Is Only a Dream" (3) "Woman Is Fickle" (4) "Lover Come Back to Me" (5) "Cossack Love Song."

    1( )   2( )   3( )   4( )   5( )

16. Potkin said that as far as women were concerned, a man should (1) give them everything they asked for (2) let them entirely alone (3) get all the kissing and cooking he could (4) watch out for them all the time (5) take them or leave them, just as he pleased.

    1( )   2( )   3( )   4( )   5( )

17. Potkin said that when any man talked about women, it reminded him of (1) the lion and the mouse (2) the king who married a peasant girl (3) the song about the farmer's daughter (4) the peasant who was angry with a city (5) the fox who could not reach the grapes.   1( )   2( )   3( )   4( )   5( )

18. Potkin said that his wife had fallen in love with him because (1) he had money (2) he was a soldier (3) he had saved her life (4) he brought her apples (5) he knocked her down.

    1( )   2( )   3( )   4( )   5( )

19. Potkin said that a man who went to the Governor's ball without an invitation would be (1) shot at sunrise (2) hanged by the thumbs (3) sent to Siberia (4) court-martialed (5) put on guard duty for a long time.   1( )   2( )   3( )   4( )   5( )

20. The count told Tanya that if she married for money, she should (1) be sure she loved the man (2) let Michael alone (3) be sure she got the money (4) forget all about love (5) get it and then do what she pleased.   1( )   2( )   3( )   4( )   5( )

21. When Tanya and Boris were in the music room, she started to leave but decided to stay if he would (1) promote Michael (2) announce their wedding soon (3) open the window (4) make love to her (5) leave the door open.

1( )   2( )   3( )   4( )   5( )

22. When Boris and Tanya were in the music room together, he said that he hoped (1) Tanya would always love him (2) he could bear to wait for the wedding (3) Michael would not cause any trouble (4) he was the man Tanya had been singing of (5) Tanya could dance as well as she sang.

1( )   2( )   3( )   4( )   5( )

23. When Michael danced with Tanya at the ball, she asked if he had come there to (1) carry her off (2) fight Boris (3) announce their engagement (4) sing (5) make a scene.

1( )   2( )   3( )   4( )   5( )

24. Tanya tried to protect Michael by saying he came to (1) protect the guests against bandits (2) wish them happiness (3) bring a message (4) return her bracelet (5) say goodbye.

1( )   2( )   3( )   4( )   5( )

25. The reward Boris offered Michael for his service to the princess was (1) a kiss from the princess (2) money (3) promotion in the army (4) a medal (5) an invitation to the wedding.

1( )   2( )   3( )   4( )   5( )

26. Michael insulted Tanya by (1) singing a song (2) getting drunk (3) dancing with her (4) coming through the window (5) kissing her.   1( )   2( )   3( )   4( )   5( )

27. When Michael went to the dance, he sang a song which said (1) "Kill your sweetheart" (2) "I want you to love me" (3) "Now is the time for love" (4) "Men are made for war" (5) "If your sweetheart leaves you, be brave."

1( )   2( )   3( )   4( )   5( )

28. Michael knew there was something wrong at Fort Darvaz because (1) he met some soldiers and loose horses (2) a message was sent to him (3) no flag was flying and the gate was open (4) there were bodies in the road (5) he heard shots and yells.

1( )   2( )   3( )   4( )   5( )

29. Michael told the native soldiers that they lacked the final mark of bravery which was the ability to (1) laugh at death (2) obey orders (3) attack at night (4) fight with swords (5) drill regularly.   1( )   2( )   3( )   4( )   5( )

30. Tanya came to the Fort to   (1) make up with Michael   (2) laugh at
    Michael   (3) warn Michael   (4) get away from Boris   (5) whip
    Michael.   1( )   2( )   3( )   4( )   5( )

31. Michael said that the Turkomans fought at close range with   (1)
    knives (2) pistols (3) clubs (4) spears (5) revolvers.
                                1( )   2( )   3( )   4( )   5( )

32. When Tanya found out the danger they were in at the Fort, she   (1)
    tried to make the soldiers fight (2) wanted to leave (3) wished
    Boris would come   (4) was glad she hurt Michael (5) told Michael
    she was sorry.   1( )   2( )   3( )   4( )   5( )

33. Before Michael went out to fight, he gave Tanya a (1) map   (2)
    rope (3) ring (4) gun (5) knife.
                                1( )   2( )   3( )   4( )   5( )

34. The soldiers refused to help Michael attack the Turkomans because
    (1) they were afraid   (2) they thought they had a better chance
    inside the Fort (3) they were afraid to follow Michael (4) they
    thought the Governor was coming with help (5) they did not want
    to leave the Fort unguarded.
                                1( )   2( )   3( )   4( )   5( )

35. When the soldiers refused to follow Michael in an attack he   (1) sang
    a song to them   (2) shot two of them   (3) gave them money   (4)
    went without them   (5) made fun of them.
                                1( )   2( )   3( )   4( )   5( )

36. The Russian soldiers attacked the Turkomans by   (1) creeping up
    from rock to rock   (2) shooting at them from long range   (3) rolling
    rocks down on them   (4) attacking on horseback   (5) making a
    bayonet charge.   1( )   2( )   3( )   4( )   5( )

37. When Boris saw Tanya and Michael riding and singing together, he
    (1) left the Fort (2) wept (3) took Tanya to her room (4) drank
    a toast to them (5) ordered his soldiers to seize Michael.
                                1( )   2( )   3( )   4( )   5( )

38. When Tanya heard Michael and the troops returning to the Fort, she
    (1) ran to meet him (2) returned to town (3) called Boris (4)
    hid (5) escaped in the opposite direction.
                                1( )   2( )   3( )   4( )   5( )

39. The count said that a military man's way of starting the day off was
    to (1) eat a steak for breakfast (2) kill his own breakfast (3)
    fire a machine gun (4) look around for enemies (5) kiss a girl.
                                1( )   2( )   3( )   4( )   5( )

40. When Tanya decided that Michael had been killed, she (1) sang a song to the soldiers (2) went to her room and cried (3) asked Boris to take her away (4) started to go and look for him (5) asked her uncle to look for him.

1( )   2( )   3( )   4( )   5( )

41. What actor did you like the best? (1) Igor (2) Tanya (3) Boris (4) Potkin (5) Michael.

1( )   2( )   3( )   4( )   5( )

42. At what time did you like Michael most? When he (1) sang to his soldiers on the boat (2) sang with the princess (3) came to the ball (4) took command of the Fort (5) led his men to the attack.

1( )   2( )   3( )   4( )   5( )

A GENERAL TEST

The questions given below are very general in type. Please answer each one the best you can, and give whatever answer you think is correct, regardless of where you learned the answer. In each sentence select the answer which you think is correct or which comes closest to being the correct one. Notice its number, and put a cross in the circle which has the same number as the correct answer. Here is a general sample.

The capital of Ohio is (1) Dayton (2) Cincinnati (3) Cleveland (4) Columbus (5) Toledo.

1( )   2( )   3( )   4(×)   5( )

In this case, Columbus, number 4, is the correct answer, so there is a cross in circle 4. *Mark only one answer for each question.*

Do not hurry. These answers do not affect your school grades; we want to find out what sort of things you are interested in as shown by what you remember about them.

Most of the following questions apply to Russia before the World War. For all these questions remember what Russian conditions were like and answer the best you can, regardless of where you learned the information.

1. A Russian army officer would be most likely to be punished for (1) kissing a girl in public (2) failing to return the salute of a private (3) being out of uniform (4) eating where his soldiers could see him (5) drinking while on duty.

1( )   2( )   3( )   4( )   5( )

2. A Russian governor who gave a dance would ask (1) the important government officials (2) all important men in the district (3) all important officials, business men, army officers and nobility (4) all the soldiers and officials (5) all the people in the district.

1( )   2( )   3( )   4( )   5( )

3. A cheap, coarse song is called (1) vulgar (2) jazz (3) popular (4) comic (5) risqué. 1( ) 2( ) 3( ) 4( ) 5( )

4. In Russia the poor people had a drink called (1) sake (2) benedictine (3) absinthe (4) ale (5) vodka.
1( ) 2( ) 3( ) 4( ) 5( )

5. The Khirgiz and Cossack tribesmen of southeastern Russia wear (1) turbans (2) round caps (3) tall hats made of sheep skin (4) tall crowned straw hats (5) handkerchiefs over their heads.
1( ) 2( ) 3( ) 4( ) 5( )

6. If a man wanted to be a high officer in the Russian army, he not only had to be capable, but also be (1) a nobleman (2) rich (3) the son of a soldier (4) the son of a tradesman (5) a peasant.
1( ) 2( ) 3( ) 4( ) 5( )

7. The ruler of Russia in 1913 was called (1) king (2) president (3) kaiser (4) dictator (5) tsar.
1( ) 2( ) 3( ) 4( ) 5( )

8. A brave Russian soldier might be decorated with the (1) Victoria Cross (2) Croix de Guerre (3) Order of Malta (4) Cross of St. Vladimir (5) Iron Cross.
1( ) 2( ) 3( ) 4( ) 5( )

9. Russian peasant women usually wore on their heads (1) lace caps (2) kerchiefs (3) straw bonnets (4) winged linen caps (5) felt hats. 1( ) 2( ) 3( ) 4( ) 5( )

10. Russian writing looks a good deal like that of (1) German (2) English (3) Swedish (4) French (5) Greek.
1( ) 2( ) 3( ) 4( ) 5( )

11. Russian soldiers wear uniforms much like (1) German soldiers (2) French colonials (3) American sailors (4) Scotch soldiers (5) Riff soldiers. 1( ) 2( ) 3( ) 4( ) 5( )

12. One body of water in Russia is the (1) Bay of Bengal (2) Caspian Sea (3) Lake Chad (4) Dead Sea (5) Bay of Biscay.
1( ) 2( ) 3( ) 4( ) 5( )

13. The religion of most of the people of Russia is (1) Roman Catholic (2) Moslem (3) Protestant (4) Greek Catholic (5) Buddhist.
1( ) 2( ) 3( ) 4( ) 5( )

14. In Russia, one of the mountain ranges is the (1) Apennines (2) Kenya (3) Chiricahua (4) Andes (5) Caucasus.
1( ) 2( ) 3( ) 4( ) 5( )

15. When a Russian army officer attended a formal dance, he usually wore   (1) a Tuxedo   (2) a full dress suit   (3) his usual uniform   (4) a dress uniform   (5) business suit.

      1( ) 2( ) 3( ) 4( ) 5( )

16. A commissioned Russian army officer showed his rank and the number of his regiment on an ornament on his   (1) shoulder   (2) arm   (3) neck   (4) breast   (5) cap.

      1( ) 2( ) 3( ) 4( ) 5( )

17. A man who tried to conquer Russia and failed was   (1) Charlemagne   (2) Napoleon   (3) Achilles   (4) Wellington   (5) Mussolini.

      1( ) 2( ) 3( ) 4( ) 5( )

18. On a Russian boat, the steerage (poorer) passengers usually amuse themselves by   (1) playing bridge   (2) listening to a concert   (3) listening to a radio   (4) dancing and singing   (5) playing games such as deck tennis.   1( ) 2( ) 3( ) 4( ) 5( )

19. Enemies who attack the Russians a great deal are the   (1) Turkomans   (2) Italians   (3) Albanians   (4) Montenegrans   (5) Swedes.

      1( ) 2( ) 3( ) 4( ) 5( )

20. A general who did not like one of his officers could get rid of him easily by   (1) putting him in prison   (2) shooting him   (3) sending him into exile   (4) giving him some very dangerous work   (5) making him get married.   1( ) 2( ) 3( ) 4( ) 5( )

21. A Russian priest would usually perform a marriage in   (1) Latin   (2) Russian   (3) English   (4) part English and part Latin   (5) Russian and Latin.   1( ) 2( ) 3( ) 4( ) 5( )

22. The number of witnesses at a wedding under the Greek Catholic faith must be at least   (1) one   (2) two   (3) three   (4) four   (5) five.   1( ) 2( ) 3( ) 4( ) 5( )

23. After a man had given a message to be sent by telegraph, the time it would take to send it is   (1) half minute   (2) about one minute   (3) several minutes   (4) half hour   (5) an hour.

      1( ) 2( ) 3( ) 4( ) 5( )

24. One language which practically no high-class Russians spoke was   (1) French   (2) German   (3) English   (4) Gypsy   (5) Slavic.

      1( ) 2( ) 3( ) 4( ) 5( )

25. A city in southeastern Russia is   (1) Krasnov   (2) Riga   (3) Tiflis   (4) Budapest   (5) Oslo.   1( ) 2( ) 3( ) 4( ) 5( )

26. If a Russian princess had gone out without a body guard, the poor people would probably have   (1) shot her   (2) made her go home   (3) done nothing to her   (4) celebrated in her honor   (5) sent for her soldiers.   1( )   2( )   3( )   4( )   5( )

27. If a Russian princess went out for a long auto ride, she would usually   (1) go by herself   (2) go only when friends or relatives were along   (3) have a military guard   (4) have a guard of detectives   (5) have only two or three servants along.   1( )   2( )   3( )   4( )   5( )

28. A Russian princess would consider a lieutenant in the army as (1) superior in rank   (2) an equal in rank   (3) a person slightly inferior in rank   (4) a high type of servant   (5) similar to a peasant.
                                                 1( )   2( )   3( )   4( )   5( )

29. When a Russian princess had become engaged, the person who announced it would have been   (1) the princess   (2) the fiancé   (3) her brother   (4) her parents   (5) the ruler of Russia.
                                                 1( )   2( )   3( )   4( )   5( )

30. One characteristic of the usual Russian wedding is   (1) a wait of several weeks after the engagement   (2) a lot of flowers   (3) a ceremony which takes all day   (4) a large orchestra   (5) a large bridal procession.   1( )   2( )   3( )   4( )   5( )

31. A Russian princess married   (1) anyone she pleased   (2) whoever her relatives selected   (3) some one approved by the ruler   (4) some one the priest would approve of   (5) an officer in the army or navy.
                                                 1( )   2( )   3( )   4( )   5( )

32. A young Russian officer who was speaking to a princess would address her   (1) "Your highness"   (2) "mademoiselle"   (3) "Duchess"   (4) "Princess"   (5) by her first name.
                                                 1( )   2( )   3( )   4( )   5( )

33. If a Russian nobleman noticed that his niece was in love with a peasant, he would probably   (1) encourage them   (2) let them alone   (3) warn the niece to let the man alone   (4) tell them he disapproved   (5) have the man punished.   1( )   2( )   3( )   4( )   5( )

34. Russian cavalrymen were usually armed with   (1) swords and knives   (2) swords and long rifles   (3) swords and short rifles   (4) short rifles and spears   (5) swords and spears.
                                                 1( )   2( )   3( )   4( )   5( )

35. When one company of soldiers is moved to another place, it usually travels under the command of a   (1) colonel   (2) major   (3) captain   (4) lieutenant   (5) sergeant.   1( )   2( )   3( )   4( )   5( )

36. In small Russian taverns there were usually *no* (1) entertainers (2) soldiers (3) dancing (4) singing (5) orchestra.
1( ) 2( ) 3( ) 4( ) 5( )

37. A small fort on the frontier would probably be in command of a (1) general (2) colonel (3) lieutenant (4) sergeant (5) corporal.
1( ) 2( ) 3( ) 4( ) 5( )

38. The best place for a fort is (1) in a wide valley (2) out on the open plain (3) built against a steep cliff (4) on top of a high hill (5) in a narrow valley.
1( ) 2( ) 3( ) 4( ) 5( )

39. A lieutenant on a steamer would (1) be free to go all over the boat (2) mingle with all passengers but royalty (3) visit freely even with royalty (4) have to remain with his soldiers (5) have to keep away from the peasants.
1( ) 2( ) 3( ) 4( ) 5( )

40. When troops left a fort to attack an enemy, they probably would (1) leave about half to protect the fort (2) all go to the attack (3) leave just one squad (4) leave one man and a machine gun (5) go after reinforcements.
1( ) 2( ) 3( ) 4( ) 5( )

41. In Russia most of the people are engaged in (1) manufacture (2) agriculture (3) mining (4) fishing (5) drilling of oil.
1( ) 2( ) 3( ) 4( ) 5( )

42. A famous Russian writer was (1) De Maupassant (2) Poe (3) Tolstoi (4) Disraeli (5) Dumas.
1( ) 2( ) 3( ) 4( ) 5( )

43. One of the principal rivers of Russia is the (1) Ganges (2) Rhone (3) Catawba (4) Euphrates (5) Volga.
1( ) 2( ) 3( ) 4( ) 5( )

44. In southeastern Russia, the people make money by (1) making felt hats (2) weaving rugs (3) mining coal (4) raising fruit (5) molding statues.
1( ) 2( ) 3( ) 4( ) 5( )

45. Before the war, Russia was divided into (1) separate kingdoms (2) many small provinces (3) two large sections (4) states such as the United States (5) a few large provinces.
1( ) 2( ) 3( ) 4( ) 5( )

"STOLEN HEAVEN"

A SPECIFIC TEST

The following sentences describe some of the action or setting of the movie. In each sentence select the answer which you think is correct or which comes closest to being the correct one. Notice its number and put a cross in the circle which has the same number as the correct answer. Here is a sample, not taken from the movie.

The capital of Ohio is (1) Dayton (2) Cincinnati (3) Cleveland (4) Columbus (5) Toledo. 1( ) 2( ) 3( ) 4(×) 5( )

In this case, Columbus, number 4, is the correct answer, so there is a cross in circle 4. *Mark only one answer for each question.*

Do not hurry. These answers do not affect your school grades; we just want to find out what you liked about the movie as shown by what you remember about it.

If you forget who was who in the picture, look at this list.

> Mary—the girl
> Joe—the husband
> Steve—a friend of Mary and Joe

1. The actress who played the lead in this picture was (1) Joan Crawford (2) Clara Bow (3) Mary Astor (4) Nancy Carroll (5) Kay Johnson. 1( ) 2( ) 3( ) 4( ) 5( )

2. At the time Joe came to Mary's room they (1) were meeting for the first time (2) had been together all evening (3) had been together since noon (4) had known each other several months (5) had known each other since childhood.
1( ) 2( ) 3( ) 4( ) 5( )

3. Joe's head was hurt by (1) broken glass (2) a policeman's club (3) a bullet (4) a rock (5) a sharp knife.
1( ) 2( ) 3( ) 4( ) 5( )

4. Mary found out that Joe's head was hurt when she (1) saw blood on his face (2) saw him wince with pain (3) noticed blood on the pillow (4) saw his torn hat (5) ran her fingers through his hair.
1( ) 2( ) 3( ) 4( ) 5( )

5. When the police found Joe in Mary's room, she told them he (1) was her brother (2) was the robber (3) had followed her home (4) was her sweetheart (5) was her husband.
1( ) 2( ) 3( ) 4( ) 5( )

6. Mary said she had lost her job as a dancer because she (1) wouldn't work late at night (2) wasn't a good enough dancer (3) weighed too much (4) wasn't liked by the customers (5) wouldn't let the manager make love to her. 1( ) 2( ) 3( ) 4( ) 5( )

7. Mary said that if she had a lot of money she would like to (1) send it back to the owners (2) buy a farm (3) buy a dress shop (4) go on a honeymoon (5) put it in the bank.
1( ) 2( ) 3( ) 4( ) 5( )

8. At the boarding house, Joe and Mary decided to spend all the money and then   (1) go to work   (2) run away   (3) go to jail   (4) kill themselves   (5) get married.   1( )   2( )   3( )   4( )   5( )

9. Mary said they had stolen not money, but   (1) music   (2) peace   (3) time   (4) books   (5) excitement.
                            1( )   2( )   3( )   4( )   5( )

10. The first scene at the hotel showed an orchestra playing   (1) "La Paloma"   (2) "Kiss Me Again"   (3) "Peanut Vendor"   (4) "Aloha"   (5) "Yours and Mine."
                             1( )   2( )   3( )   4( )   5( )

11. The first time Steve was interested in Mary was when he saw her   (1) on the beach   (2) at dinner   (3) at a party   (4) swimming   (5) dancing.   1( )   2( )   3( )   4( )   5( )

12. Joe thought all the bell-boys were afraid of them because   (1) he was tall and strong   (2) he gave big tips   (3) he and Mary were young   (4) their trunks were new and heavy   (5) he and Mary were on their honeymoon.   1( )   2( )   3( )   4( )   5( )

13. At the hotel, Joe bought Mary a   (1) coat   (2) auto   (3) dog   (4) dress   (5) necklace.   1( )   2( )   3( )   4( )   5( )

14. The detective decided Joe and Mary had gone South as   (1) they bought some trunks   (2) they bought new overcoats   (3) he found out what kind of clothes they bought   (4) the landlady heard where they were going   (5) he found out they bought tickets for Palm Beach.
                             1( )   2( )   3( )   4( )   5( )

15. The first time Steve made love to Mary they were   (1) having lunch   (2) dancing   (3) on the beach   (4) at a party   (5) in Mary's room.
                             1( )   2( )   3( )   4( )   5( )

16. On the beach, Joe was afraid because   (1) Steve talked to Mary a long time   (2) he met a police commissioner   (3) Mary wanted to play with the baby   (4) Mary asked him for some money   (5) he heard that detectives were after him.
                             1( )   2( )   3( )   4( )   5( )

17. At the hotel, their room cost per day   (1) $5   (2) $7.50   (3) $12   (4) $20   (5) $50.   1( )   2( )   3( )   4( )   5( )

18. At the hotel Joe said they would not be able to go to a dance on the following Wednesday because   (1) they would be too poor at that time   (2) they wouldn't be there   (3) he would be arrested before then   (4) he didn't want to go to Steve's   (5) they were going to another party.   1( )   2( )   3( )   4( )   5( )

19. In the hotel room, Joe said that he and Mary would see each other again   (1) in the hospital   (2) in jail   (3) in heaven   (4) after they got out of jail   (5) when Mary got back from her trip.

    1( )   2( )   3( )   4( )   5( )

20. Mary said that if Joe shot himself she would   (1) spend all the money that was left   (2) go off with Steve   (3) go back to New York   (4) give herself up to the police   (5) kill herself also.

    1( )   2( )   3( )   4( )   5( )

21. Joe said he probably would not be strong enough to dance because (1) Mary had kissed him   (2) his head hurt badly   (3) he had not eaten any dinner   (4) he swam too far   (5) he was too sunburned.

    1( )   2( )   3( )   4( )   5( )

22. When Mary found out that most of the money was gone, she asked Joe for the rest, and said she intended to   (1) save it   (2) spend it all in one night   (3) gamble with it   (4) spread it as far as it would go (5) send it back.

    1( )   2( )   3( )   4( )   5( )

23. Mary called herself   (1) "On the Spot" Mary   (2) "Rough and Ready" Mary   (3) "Get the Cash" Mary   (4) "Shoot the Works" Mary   (5) "Never Say Die" Mary.

    1( )   2( )   3( )   4( )   5( )

24. Joe saw that Steve liked Mary, and he asked Steve to   (1) take care of her   (2) take her away   (3) leave her alone   (4) send her home (5) pay her bills.

    1( )   2( )   3( )   4( )   5( )

25. When the money was almost gone, Mary tried to make some more by (1) vamping Steve   (2) having Steve gamble for her   (3) gambling for herself   (4) dancing in the hotel café   (5) playing in the orchestra.

    1( )   2( )   3( )   4( )   5( )

26. At the dance, Mary was worried because Joe said that he intended to (1) go to his room   (2) shoot Steve   (3) leave town   (4) give up to the police   (5) go to work.

    1( )   2( )   3( )   4( )   5( )

27. Steve said he would help Mary if she would   (1) be sure and pay him back   (2) kiss him   (3) always love her husband   (4) go to Havana with him   (5) give up to the police.

    1( )   2( )   3( )   4( )   5( )

28. When Mary was at the dance, she went over to the orchestra and started playing   (1) a piano   (2) the drums   (3) a saxophone   (4) a slide whistle   (5) a violin.

    1( )   2( )   3( )   4( )   5( )

29. Joe started to shoot himself because he (1) thought Mary didn't love him (2) was sorry he had stolen the money (3) was afraid the police would arrest him (4) had spent all his money (5) thought Steve was about to report him to the police.

    1( ) 2( ) 3( ) 4( ) 5( )

30. When Mary took the money to Joe she said, (1) "We had better pay our debts" (2) "It's just like we had never taken the money" (3) "Let's go on having a good time" (4) "Let's go back to our jobs" (5) "I'm leaving with Steve." 1( ) 2( ) 3( ) 4( ) 5( )

31. When the policeman arrested Joe and Mary in the hotel, he looked for (1) the scar on Joe's head (2) Joe's gun (3) the money (4) the things they had bought (5) Mary's jewelry.

    1( ) 2( ) 3( ) 4( ) 5( )

32. When the policeman put handcuffs on Mary and Joe, Mary covered up the handcuffs with (1) a scarf (2) her coat (3) Joe's overcoat (4) a newspaper (5) a blanket. 1( ) 2( ) 3( ) 4( ) 5( )

33. In the hotel, Joe and Mary got away from the policeman because (1) the lights were turned out (2) Steve helped them get away (3) two drunken men started a fight (4) Mary threw some money in the air (5) Mary tripped the policeman. 1( ) 2( ) 3( ) 4( ) 5( )

34. After they escaped from the hotel, Mary told their chair-man to stop somewhere so that they could (1) listen to the radio (2) buy some stamps (3) get a newspaper (4) buy some candy (5) get the hand-cuffs off. 1( ) 2( ) 3( ) 4( ) 5( )

35. When Mary and Joe arrived at Steve's house, their handcuffs were removed by (1) Steve (2) Joe (3) Mary (4) Steve's butler (5) the detective. 1( ) 2( ) 3( ) 4( ) 5( )

36. When Mary and Joe met Steve at his house, Steve told Joe to (1) go hide somewhere (2) give himself up (3) return the money (4) swim out to his boat (5) take a truck and drive away.

    1( ) 2( ) 3( ) 4( ) 5( )

37. When Joe and Mary heard Steve's signal from the boat, they did not answer because (1) Mary was afraid of Steve (2) they saw the police (3) Mary decided it was better to go to jail (4) they thought it was a trap (5) Joe didn't want Mary to be with Steve.

    1( ) 2( ) 3( ) 4( ) 5( )

38. The main reason Joe was sorry he had stolen the money was that (1) he thought he had done the wrong thing (2) Mary might be accused of taking it (3) he was afraid to meet new people (4) he would have to go to prison (5) the police were after him all the time.

    1( ) 2( ) 3( ) 4( ) 5( )

39. When Mary and Joe met Steve on the beach, she gave him (1) a kiss (2) a handkerchief (3) the envelope of money (4) her coat (5) a ring. 1( ) 2( ) 3( ) 4( ) 5( )

40. The reason Steve told the policeman he would help Joe get free from the charge was (1) Steve was in love with Mary (2) Steve thought Joe was innocent (3) Mary had paid money for his help (4) Steve owed Joe some money (5) Steve expected Mary to go with him. 1( ) 2( ) 3( ) 4( ) 5( )

41. At the close of the picture, we saw Joe arrested for stealing the money. He was probably (1) set free (2) freed on probation (3) put in jail for a couple of years (4) put in jail for ten or fifteen years (5) hanged. 1( ) 2( ) 3( ) 4( ) 5( )

42. At what point in the picture did you like Mary the best? When she (1) took in a man off the street (2) hid a man from the police (3) gambled away the last thousand dollars (4) accepted the money from Steve (5) told Joe they would go to jail to pay for the crime. 1( ) 2( ) 3( ) 4( ) 5( )

43. In what part of the picture did you like Joe the best? When he (1) was able to rob the factory (2) got away from the police (3) started to shoot himself (4) asked another man to take care of Mary (5) decided to give back the money. 1( ) 2( ) 3( ) 4( ) 5( )

APPENDIX II

BIBLIOGRAPHY

1. BALCOLM, A. G.: "The Film as a Medium of Instruction," *Journal of National Education Association*, 1924, 13, 331–332.
2. BALLARD, PHILIP BOSWOOD: "Obliviscence and Reminiscence," *British Journal of Psychology Monograph Supplements*, 1913, 1, No. 2, pp. vii, 82.
3. BASSETT, SARAH JANET: "Retention of History in the Sixth, Seventh and Eighth Grades with Special Reference to the Factors that Influence Retention," *Johns Hopkins University Studies in Education*, 1928, No. 12, pp. viii, 110.
4. BEAN, C. H.: "The Curve of Forgetting," *Archives of Psychology*, 1912, 3, No. 21, pp. iii, 45.
5. BROWN, WARNER: "Effects of Interval on Recall," *Journal of Experimental Psychology*, 1924, 7, 469–474.
6. CHARCOT, JEAN MARTIN: *Leçons sur les Maladies due Système Nerveux*, 3 vols. Paris: Bureau du Progrès Médical, 1890–1894.
7. CONRAD, HERBERT S., and JONES, HAROLD ELLIS: *Psychological Studies of Motion Pictures. III: Fidelity of Report as a Measure of Adult Intelligence*, University of California Publications in Psychology, 1918–1929 (1929, No. 7), 3, 245–276.
8. DALLENBACH, KARL M.: "The Measurement of Attention," *American Journal of Psychology*, 1913, 24, 465–507.
9. EBBINGHAUS, HERMANN: *Memory: A Contribution to Experimental Psychology*, translated by Henry A. Ruger and Clara E. Bussenius. New York: Teachers College, Columbia University, 1913, pp. iii, viii, 123.
10. *Educational Screen*, files from 1924 (Vol. 3) to date.
11. FINKENBINDER, E. O.: "The Curve of Forgetting," *American Journal of Psychology*, 1913, 24, 8–32.
12. GARRETT, HENRY E.: *Statistics in Psychology and Education*. New York: Longmans, Green, 1926, pp. xiii, 317.
13. HENDERSON, E. N.: "A Study of Memory for Connected Trains of Thought," *Psychological Review Monograph Supplement*, 1903, 5, No. 6, pp. iv, 94.
14. JONES, HAROLD ELLIS; CONRAD, HERBERT; and HORN, AARON: *Psychological Studies of Motion Pictures. II: Observation and Re-*

call as a Function of Age, University of California Publications in Psychology, 1918–1929 (1928, No. 6), 3, 225–243.

15. KUHLMANN, F.: "On the Analysis of the Memory Consciousness for Pictures of Familiar Objects," *American Journal of Psychology,* 1907, 18, 389–420.

16. LACY, JOHN V.: "The Relative Value of Motion Pictures as an Educational Agency: An Experimental Study," *Teachers College Record,* 1919, 20, 452–465.

17. LEE, ANG LANFEN: "An Experimental Study of Retention and Its Relation to Intelligence," *Psychological Monographs,* 1925, 34, No. 4, pp. x, 45.

18. LUH, C. W.: "The Conditions of Retention," *Psychological Monographs,* 1922, 31, No. 3, pp. 87.

19. MCGEOCH, JOHN A., and WHITELY, PAUL L.: "The Recall of Observed Material," *Journal of Educational Psychology,* 1926, 17, 419–425.

20. MEUMANN, E.: *The Psychology of Learning: An Experimental Investigation of the Economy and Technique of Memory,* translated by John Wallace Baird. New York: D. Appleton [c. 1913], pp. xix, 393.

21. MITCHELL, ALICE MILLER: *Children and Movies.* Chicago: University of Chicago Press, 1929, pp. xxiv, 181.

22. MÜLLER, GEORG ELIAS: *Zur Analyse der Gedächtnistätigkeit und des Vorstellungsverlaufes,* 3 vols. Leipzig: J. A. Barth, 1911–1917.

23. MÜLLER, G. E., and SCHIEMANN, F.: *Experimentelle Beitrage zur Untersuchung des Gedächtnisse.* Hamburg: Voss, 1893.

24. PORTER, ELFA MCWILLIAM: *The Curve of Retention in Moving Pictures for Young Children.* State University of Iowa, unpublished master's thesis, 1930, pp. 119.

25. RADOSSAWLJEWITSCH, P. R.: *Das Behalten und Vergessen bei Kindern und Erwachsenen nach Experimentellen Untersuchungen* (Das Fortschreiten des Vergessens mit der Zeit). Leipzig: Nemnich, 1907, pp. 197.

26. ROGERS, ROWLAND: "Cutting the Time of Learning," *Educational Screen,* 1925, 4, 13–14.

27. RUCH, G. M.: *The Objective or New-Type Examination: An Introduction to Educational Measurement.* Chicago: Scott, Foresman [c. 1929], pp. x, 478.

28. RUCH, G. M., and STODDARD, GEORGE D.: *Tests and Measurements in High School Instruction.* Yonkers-on-Hudson, N. Y.: World Book Co., 1927, pp. xix, 381.

29. SEABURY, WILLIAM MARSTON: *The Public and the Motion Picture Industry.* New York: Macmillan, 1926, pp. xiv, 340.

30. SEABURY, WILLIAM MARSTON: *Motion Picture Problems: The Cinema and the League of Nations.* New York: Avondale Press, 1929, pp. 426.

31. STARCH, DANIEL: *Educational Psychology.* New York: Macmillan, 1928, pp. ix, 568.

32. STECKER, H. DORA: "Children and the Moving Pictures: As Seen from the Box Office," *Child Welfare Magazine*, 1928–1929, 23, 59–62; 130–132.

33. THORNDIKE, EDWARD L.: *Educational Psychology. Vol. II: The Psychology of Learning.* New York: Teachers College, Columbia University [c. 1913], pp. xi, 452 (pp. 305–331).

34. WEBER, JOSEPH J.: "Bibliography on the Use of Visual Aids in Education," *Educational Screen*, 1930, 9, 29–31; 61–63; 93–95; 123–127; 155–159; 187–191.

35. WHITELY, PAUL L., and McGEOCH, JOHN A.: "The Curve of Retention for Poetry," *Journal of Educational Psychology*, 1928, 19, 471–479.

36. WILLIAMS, OSBORNE: "A Study of the Phenomenon of Reminiscence," *Journal of Experimental Psychology*, 1926, 9, 368–387.

INDEX